The Littlest Learners

The Littlest Learners

Preparing Your Child
for Kindergarten

Dawn R. Roginski

ROWMAN & LITTLEFIELD
Lanham • Boulder • New York • London

Published by Rowman & Littlefield
A wholly owned subsidiary of The Rowman & Littlefield Publishing Group, Inc.
4501 Forbes Boulevard, Suite 200, Lanham, Maryland 20706
www.rowman.com

Unit A, Whitacre Mews, 26-34 Stannary Street, London SE11 4AB

British Library Cataloguing in Publication Information Available

Library of Congress Cataloging-in-Publication Data Available

ISBN: 978-1-4758-3276-1 (cloth : alk. paper)
ISBN: 978-1-4758-3298-5 (electronic)

Printed in the United States of America

I have been so blessed to be surrounded by a love of language and literacy. Without my wonderful role models my career may never have become a passion. And so, this book is for you:

To my parents, Richard and Nancy Turocy, thank you for the loving words that always filled my ears and our home.

To my children, *Rachel, Leah, and Alex*, thank you for understanding that a family that talks, reads, and plays together is a family that will love together.

To *Bob*, thank you for surrounding me with the silence I needed to complete this title. Your silent encouragement is one of my favorite blessings.

To the many *educators* not only from my academic career, but those of my children, thank you for providing me an opportunity to watch from afar. Your dedication and commitment to your craft often goes unseen. When you feel you are underappreciated, please recognize that your efforts are forever shaping the future and many are grateful.

Contents

Preface

There are many milestones that cause every parent's heart to start beating rapidly. Sharing the initial news that one is expecting a child is instantly exciting and terrifying. Expectant parents worry about labor, delivery, and their abilities to be a good parent. They may worry that their child won't be able to compete with that baby down the block. Perhaps their neighbor attends Little Gym® activities, Itsy Bitsy Yoga®, and Kindermusik® programs. A new parent may fret that her child will not be the best. The need to be competitive is reinforced when the expectant mom registers for her baby shower. She is bombarded not only by strollers, car seats, and cribs but also "must-have" activity mats, baby-safe puzzles, Leap Frog® educational toys, and Baby Einstein® multimedia products. A mother-to-be may even hear rumblings that the wait-list for the "best" preschool fills up before her to-be-preschooler has even arrived. A well-intentioned mommy may feel a need to get her baby-to-be on that wait-list lest she be too late.

A frenzied new mom may wonder if she will have the time to simply rock her baby while singing a soft lullaby. She may question if reading picture books out loud is ever going to prepare her child for that competitive preschool. She may wonder if the nursery rhymes she remembers from her own childhood are now too outdated to share with her baby. Mom may speculate that allowing her youngster to play with spatulas and bowls is wasting precious teaching time. She may also question if buying mass-marketed products is the best way to guarantee her child's future literacy and eventual success.

Once parents have survived infancy, toddlerhood, and preschool, the word "kindergarten" quickly rekindles both excitement and anxiety. Parents worry that their child might not be ready to separate and miss them too much during the school day. They are also concerned that their child doesn't miss them enough. Will their child be liked by their classmate? More importantly, will they be liked by the teacher? Today, in a time when core curriculums and early learning standards make headlines, parents anguish whether they have best prepared their child for school success.

As I look back nostalgically on my own children's school careers, I recall field trips, choir concerts, art shows, Thanksgiving Day feasts, and Hundred Day celebrations. But, I would struggle to correctly name each grade's teacher. If I did recall a teacher's name, I may confuse which of my children she/he taught. While many elementary school memories are blurry, one parent-teacher conference remains crystal clear. It is that ten-minute conference that spurred my interest in emergent literacy. It is that wee conversation that shaped my career. It also triggered my need to write this book and share the culmination of my discoveries about our littlest learners.

I was realizing my own parenting anxiety as I entered a fall parent-teacher conference for my oldest daughter. She was a bright little girl (and continues to be an intelligent young woman) and I suspected that kindergarten was not terribly challenging for her. She knew not only her alphabets, numerals, shapes, and colors but was also beginning to read on her own. As a well-intentioned young parent, I asked her kindergarten teacher what I should be doing at home to continue to challenge my young student. I was shocked when the teacher responded. She said, "Don't worry mom, you did a great job with your daughter. She is on the right path and I suspect she will be a super student throughout her years. Relax. Your job is done."

In all honesty I must admit that I was terribly disappointed to not be offered a stack of worksheets and enrichment activities. I was a teacher and a librarian after all! I knew that all sorts of products were available to enrich children. I pondered why this well-respected and experienced kindergarten teacher considered my parenting job complete. I was just starting to catch on to this parenting thing, I thought! My daughter had only just turned five. What was I to do for twelve more school years? How could I continue to propel my child onto a trajectory of school success?

As I now understand, that wise woman and early learning expert was absolutely correct. My daughter continued to be a stellar student. She achieved what most would consider academic success. What exactly happened in a child's young life that her future success could be predicted by her very first classroom teacher? I have now come to believe that our kindergarten teacher wasn't simply speculating. She did have research to support her observations and suspicions about kindergarten students. As one example, the Northwest Evaluation Association indicates that virtually the entire achievement gap in language and almost 70 percent of the achievement gap in mathematics is created before the beginning of second grade and most likely between birth and kindergarten.[1]

My daughter's conference was many years ago but remains in the forefront of my mind. As a result of that very brief parent-teacher conference, I not only relaxed as a parent but have spent my resulting career in education and early literacy trying to understand what precisely needs to happen BEFORE a child enters school to assure that they are *ready* to learn. Contributing to my conclusions,

- I have provided story times in hundreds of preschools, daycare, and Head Start classrooms.
- I have conversed, shared stories, and played with hundreds of thousands of little ones.
- I have witnessed that every child has the potential to become a successful learner.
- I have conferred with thousands of parents and caregivers about the home literacy environment they have created for their family.
- I have identified and replicated the activities in my daughter's life that so pleased her kindergarten teacher and ultimately predicted her academic future.

I agree with that amazing kindergarten teacher and the early childhood world in general that a child's window of opportunity to learn language opens early in life. That open window is not intended to be with store-bought resources and a competition to race through flashcards and a prescribed early learning curriculum. Instead, parents should strive to make the most of every experience they share with their young child. Quality experiences will lead children and parents into conversation. Over time, those interactive conversations will lead to the acquisition of language. A world filled with words is a world filled with literacy. As parents and caregivers expose their children to the world and the print that fills it, they are engaging in literacy activities. Parents can steer infancy and childhood into a time of wonder and discovery. They can fill the early years with talking and listening. It is through playful discoveries and conversations that literacy and, ultimately, school success will emerge. This book will help parents and caregivers maximize those opportunities.

If you are a parent, grandparent, or caregiver of a child you hold on your lap ... this book is for you.

If you believe that children benefit from spoken and written language beginning at birth ... this book is for you.

If you believe that the activities you share with your child from infancy onward are critical in developing their future reading ability ... this book is for you.

If you wish you knew what you could do with the young child in your life that would set them on a lifelong learning journey ... this book is for you.

Photo 1.   *My successful kindergarten graduate with an amazing educator who continues to spread ripples of her wisdom to infinity. Photo courtesy of the author, reprinted with permission.*

Regardless of how you read this book, your childcare experience will be less pressured and richer for having done so. The activities in this book do not require licensed teachers, psychologists, or expensive prepackaged programs. Instead, they take what parents already do with their children and highlight the literacy experiences innately built into them: talking, reading, playing, and exploring the world.

Thank you for allowing me to share the power and joy of reading, talking, singing, and playing with children. It is my wish that this book provides you with inspiration, hours of family fun, and many memorable moments. Savor every moment, your first kindergarten parent-teacher conference is right around the corner.

NOTE

1. L. Fielding, "Kindergarten Learning Gap," *American School Board Journal* (April 2006): 32–34.

Introduction

A Starting Point

It is a widely held belief that the experiences children have from birth through age five determine not only their readiness for kindergarten but their entire academic career. Statistically, we know that the children who enter kindergarten with a sound foundation in early literacy skills will be the most successful students. When children enter kindergarten behind their peers, the kindergarten teacher is forced to squeeze seven years of learning into that child so that he will be on track to achieve the Third Grade Reading Guarantee. That task is nearly impossible for even the most skilled of kindergarten teachers. Quite simply, if a child starts behind, they will not catch up. Unfortunately, they are most likely to retain their place in the back of the class. It is proven that

- Children who enter kindergarten being read to at least three times per week show a greater phonemic awareness and are twice as likely to score in the top 25 percent in reading readiness.[1]
- Children who are poor readers in first grade demonstrate a 90 percent probability of becoming struggling readers in fourth grade.
- Children who are "ready to read" at kindergarten entrance are most likely to be reading on grade level in the second grade. It follows that children who are reading on grade level in second grade are most likely to graduate from high school. Perhaps most importantly, students who receive a high school diploma are less likely to become teen parents, incarcerated, and/or dependent on public assistance.[2]

Academic progress is so predictable that Texas looks to fourth grade reading scores to project the number of prison cells they're going to need in ten years. While the formula for projecting the necessity of jail cells is multifaceted, the general statement is not completely inaccurate. Sixty percent of

America's prison inmates are illiterate, and 85 percent of all juvenile offenders have reading problems. The percentage of prisoners in the two lowest levels of reading proficiency is 70 percent.[3] Texas isn't the only state that uses the number of elementary school students with reading difficulties as a predictor for serious problems later in life.

In order to maximize the best experiences we manufacture for our children, we need to gain a rudimentary understanding of neuroscience. Thanks to Positron Emission Tomography, or PET scans, scientists have been able to observe not only the structure of a child's brain, but more importantly the

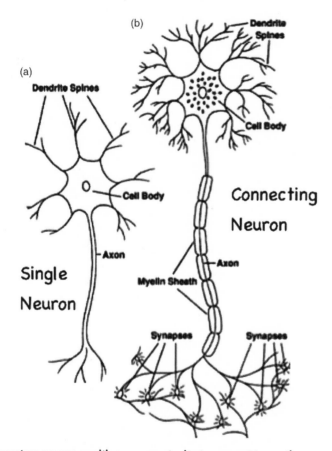

(a) An immature neuron awaiting an opportunity to connect to another neuron. (b) An example of a neuron preparing to connect to another. As neurons connect, the brain's framework becomes thicker and stronger. Illustration used courtesy of *Rethinking the Brain: New Insights into Early Development* by Rima Shore (New York: Families and Work Institute, 1997).

activity that is taking place within it. Combined with recordings of children engaged in various activities, neuroscientists can make conclusions about the interactions on the brain's actual activity. When we visualize all that is happening in our little one's brain, our decisions to incorporate language into their lives becomes second nature. We must first accept that the human brain at birth is remarkably pliable and greatly influenced by everyday happenings. No two brains are identical. Even before birth, an individual's brain is being affected by environmental conditions as well as the stimulation it is receiving. The infant's brain is affected not only by the physical care and nourishment it receives but by the mental stimulation as well. The idea of "wiring" is an analogy often used to explain the brain network. Our brain's ability to think and learn depends on the passage of signals from one part of the brain to another. The stronger the brain is wired, the more rapidly and efficiently the signal is transmitted. Just like other organs, our brain is made up of individual cells called neurons. In order for a signal to travel through our brain, the signal must transfer from one neuron to the next. Synapses, or connections, are built between neurons. One individual neuron may be connected to thousands of others. All of these synapses link together to form complex neural pathways.

We all have a finite number of neurons. We are born with more neurons than we will need. In a child's early years, they form twice as many synapses than needed. The surplus of unused synapses, those that are not reinforced repeatedly, are gradually eliminated throughout childhood and into adolescence. Once shed, those neurons (brain cells) are gone forever. The more neurons we retain, the easier a message or signal crosses the synapse. Strong synapses become exempt from elimination. In this way, a young child's experiences, positive or negative, shape the brain. And, as we now know, connected neurons build a stronger brain.

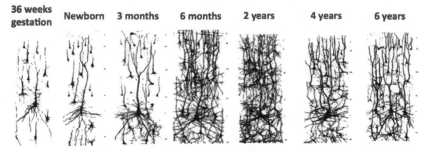

36 weeks gestation   Newborn   3 months   6 months   2 years   4 years   6 years

At birth all babies are born with virtually the same number of brain cells (neurons). Through early childhood, experiences connect neurons together to build a foundation for learning. Beginning at about age six through puberty, neurons that have not connected to another are shed and disappear forever.

Healthy brain development implies intellectual development. As such, one might assume stimulation is best achieved through toys and stimulation. Caregivers need to be cautioned that toy manufacturers who promise better brain development with the use of their product are making unfounded claims. They are in fact directly at odds with neuroscientists who have proven that warm and responsive relationships are the key to positive brain development. Children who live in print-rich environments and are read to early in life are likely to learn to read on schedule. Early reading readiness equates to being able to learn in general. Students are promoted to the next grade based on their ability to digest the year's curriculum. Much of that understanding must come from the student's ability to read the content independently.

When we understand that we are creating our child's physical brain circuitry, we undoubtedly recognize the importance of our child's earliest days. While genes dominate the approximate number of neurons in our brain at birth, retaining those neurons through the pruning process of adolescence is completely dependent on our environment and experiences.[4] The stronger our neural network, the quicker new information travels across our brain pathways. Quicker speed from one neuron to the next (across the synapses) makes it easier to learn.[5] When our neural pathways are efficient, we can learn with relatively little effort. A brain ready to learn is ready for kindergarten. While the early years are prime for brain building, it is never too late to improve the quality of a child's life. Children who do not benefit from good health and experiences in the early years can make some recovery with ongoing efforts. The brain's ability to recover and alter itself is most successful in the first decade of life. Early intense intervention is the key to overcoming an adverse childhood.

Words are fundamentally the building blocks for learning. Children accumulate their word knowledge through sight and hearing. As most children will not be independent readers until age seven or eight, the best way to fill a young pliable brain with words is through their sense of hearing. Fortunately, listening comprehension comes before reading comprehension. A child can understand a word they hear before they can use that same word in their own speech. Once they have heard and said a word, they are more likely to be able to comprehend (read) that word in a written context. A child's mind is like an empty gas tank. A parent's responsibility is to fill that tank with so much fuel (words) that the brain is powered to learn. The more fuel put into the tank, the farther the tank can travel. The farther the tank travels, the more opportunities there are to fill it up with more fuel. The ultimate time for a fill-up is in the first few years of life when the tank is primed to accept the fuel. The fuel is words—through conversation, song, and reading.

At birth the human brain is 25 percent of adult volume. By age three it is at 85 percent of its adult volume.[6] Between conception and age three, the brain is not only growing in size, it is also undergoing significant neural activity. See figure 0.1a and b.

Statistics demonstrate that academic success is fairly predictable. Yet, all children have different temperaments and develop at a pace that varies. Regardless of timing, all children with early positive language experiences can succeed. We can assert that the children who ultimately achieve academic success are similar as they enter their kindergarten classrooms. Their kindergarten teachers will report that these achievers

- enjoy being read to
- are able to retell a story
- are able to identify twelve to fifteen upper and lowercase letters (and their sounds)
- can recite five to six nursery rhymes
- can identify ending sounds (rhymes) and create rhymes of their own
- can identify beginning sounds that are alike (alliteration)
- speak in complete sentences
- have a vocabulary of four thousand to five thousand words.[7] See figure 0.2.

Literacy is the ability to read, write, speak, and gain meaning from symbols. Literacy does not just emerge naturally and there is not a specified time in a child's life when he is magically literate. Children learn in the context of their intimate relationships. Children with secure attachments early in life grow into curious and confident learners. Positive early stimulation facilitates the process of becoming literate. Learning about language occurs naturally as part of a child's daily life. "Early literacy" is the critical time in a child's development before they can conventionally read what others have written and write so that others can understand and read what they have written. All infants are born ready to learn about literacy and language. Their path to becoming readers and writers is termed "emergent literacy." From day one, infants are hearing how language is used. Babies see text surrounding them and watch as those they love use print in a world they are so curious about. When parents coordinate language-filled experiences with their child, they are facilitating early literacy and emergent reading behaviors.

Emergent literacy skills (or behaviors) have been summarized to include the following:

- Print Motivation: having an interest in and the experience of enjoying books (to love books).
- Print Awareness: the ability to notice print and an awareness of book handling behaviors (to see words).

- Letter Knowledge: the awareness that letters are everywhere and that letters have names (to see letters).
- Phonological Awareness: the ability to hear (and manipulate) the smaller sounds in words (to hear sounds).
- Vocabulary: the ability to name things (to know words).
- Narrative Skill: the ability to describe events and to tell a story (to know stories).[8]

The first four of these skills are defined by literacy experts as being "constrained skills." Simply put, these skills are developed only during early childhood. Young children who do not acquire a love of books, notice words and letters in their environment, and hear individual sounds of language will struggle to ever do so. The window of opportunity to develop these constrained skills closes around the same time children enter kindergarten. These skills are dependent on our environment and experiences. They cannot be taught. Our vocabulary and narrative skills are "unconstrained skills." We continue to develop these skills throughout our lives. We are continually adding new words to our vocabulary bank and becoming better storytellers. The larger our vocabulary when we start school, the better reader we will become. School success depends on our reading ability, and so exposure to books is critical in early childhood when early literacy behaviors are garnered.

When public librarians assumed the role as a child's first teacher, the six skills listed above were widely publicized and encouraged by a joint effort of the Public Library Association® (PLA) and the American Library Association® (ALA). Children's librarians used library story time to define the six early literacy skills and advocate their acquisition to parents, caregivers, and early childhood teachers. Librarians purposely modeled using books to expose children to the emergent literacy skills through the activities implicit in story times: books, songs, and fingerplays. In 2001 this parent education initiative became known as Every Child Ready to Read®.[9]

In 2011 PLA and ALA introduced a revision of Every Child Ready to Read, ECRR2®.[10] While this initiative continued to focus on implementing the six early literacy skills, the focus shifted to the how. What should parents, caregivers, and teachers do to best expose children to the six critical skills? ECRR2® subsequently identified the five best practices to use when explicitly engaging young children in the six critical early literacy skills. Children are most receptive when caregivers engage with them through the following:

- talking
- singing
- reading
- writing
- playing.

All five practices encourage parents to fill their young child's developing brain with words. Words experienced with a treasured loved one form those neural connections. While all of the five practices are word and language driven, reading to our children is the single *best* activity we can do for their young and growing brain. Children's picture books have been demonstrated to contain the most number of rare words per thousand.[11] In addition to facilitating the six early literacy skills of ECRR1®, when we share books with infants and young children, they also

- learn how language is used,
- learn what written language looks like,
- learn why print is used,
- learn to focus their eyes,
- learn to recognize objects, and
- experience the physical pleasure of a book-sharing experience.

When we read to infants, they are attending to the calmness and familiarity of our voice. As our infant grows, he is associating the book-sharing experience with security. A pleasurable connection between the child and the book is built. Just as children must develop the desire to become a dancer or football player, they must also develop a desire to become a reader. The caregiver who reads to their young child is forming a connection in that child's brain that reading and books are gratifying, worthwhile, and important.

Language stimulation has a direct impact on developing the "prereading" skills and ultimately reading ability. Every reading experience and conversation we have with our young child ignites the neural circuits in their brains. Because we know our children and their routines the best, we, as parents and caregivers, are positioned to maximize their emergent literacy. The simple pleasure of talking with or reading to our child secures their future school achievement while enriching their daily life.

While parents are the first and most effective teachers of their children, in 2002 the federal government passed the No Child Left Behind (NCLB) Act®. This law requires that preschools who receive federal funds be accountable for the academic progress of its students. If the NCLB Act® was to hold schools responsible for progress and boost preschool skills, the standards for success needed to be itemized. As a precursor to the current Early Childhood Learning Standards, the federal government defined the skills listed in figure 0.3 as the literacy benchmarks for the children attending federally funded preschool programs. Upon examination, the benchmarks correlate directly to the six early literacy skills highlighted by the Every Child Ready to Read® initiative.

Recently, the NCLB Act® gave way to the Every Student Succeeds Act which was signed in 2015 by President Barack Obama. This act reauthorizes the Elementary and Secondary Education Act to create a long-term, stable federal policy that gives states flexibility and encourages innovation in public education while still holding them accountable for the results. While states must stay aligned with federal standards, they are no longer required to adopt a specific core curriculum or assessment system. As a result, states are working diligently to adopt Early Childhood Learning Standards.

Every child must:

- Recognize books by cover
- Pretend to read books
- Demonstrate an understanding of how to physically handle a book
- Enter into a book sharing routine
- Make vocalizations in their crib (bed)
- Verbally label objects they see in a book
- Verbally comment on the characters they see in a book
- Demonstrate an understanding that pictures in books represent real objects outside of the book
- Be able to listen to a story
- Request an adult to read a book to them (in words or by bringing them a book to share)
- Attend to print
- Show purpose in scribbling
- Distinguish between writing and drawing
- Insert "letter like" symbols into their scribbles

Preschool Literacy Benchmarks as defined by the No Child Left Behind Act, 2002.

The states are busy adopting Early Learning Guidelines (ELGs) or standards that define what children should know (understand) and do across multiple domains of learning at specific ages. These ELGs are defined for infants, toddlers, and young children. Most ELGs are broad enough to allow for normal variation in development. The common domains of learning typically include social-emotional, language, cognitive, motor, and approaches to learning. These ELGs are designed to allow a logical progression into kindergarten and allow for appropriate assessment. When implemented well, ELGs hold to improve the odds that preschool programs will boost kindergarten readiness and set a strong foundation for future school success. Head Start, the federally funded preschool program, set forward their Head Start Early Learning Outcomes Framework (HSELOF) in 2015. The framework is based on the Head Start measures put forward in the 1998 amended Head Start Act. The framework is composed of eight domains, twenty-seven domain elements, and many specific indicators for measuring children's skills, abilities, knowledge, and behaviors. Language Development Indicators and Literacy Indicators for three to five year olds are listed below in figure 0.4.

Domain: Language and Literacy	
Sub-Domain: Attending and Understanding	
Goal P-LC 1	Child attends to communication and language from others.
Goal P-LC 2	Chid understands and responds to increasingly complex communication and language from others.
Sub:Domain: Communicating and Listening	
Goal P-LC 3	Child varies the amount information provided o meet the demands of the situation
Goal P-LC 4	Child understands, follows and uses appropriate social and conversational rules.
Goal P-LC 5	Child expresses self in increasingly long, detailed, and sophisticated ways.
Sub-Domain: Vocabulary	
Goal P-LC 6	Child understands and uses a wide variety of words for a variety of purposes.
Goal P-LC 7	Child shows understanding of word categories and relationships among words.
Domain: Literacy	
Sub-Domain: Phonological Awareness	
Goal P-LIT 1	Child demonstrates awareness that spoken language is comprised of smaller segments of sound.
Sub-Domain: Print and Alphabet Knowledge	
Goal P-LIT 2	Child demonstrates an understanding of how print is used (functions of print) and the rules that govern how print works (conventions of print).
Goal P-LIT 3	Child identifies letters of the alphabet and produces correct sounds associated with letters.
Sub-Domain: Comprehension and Text Structure	
Goal P-LIT 4	Child demonstrates an understanding of narrative structure through story telling/re-telling.
Goal P-LIT 5	Child asks and answers questions about a book that was read aloud.
Sub-Domain: Writing	
Goal P-LIT 6	Child writes for a variety of purposes using increasingly purposeful marks.

The Head Start Child Outcomes Framework for Language and Literacy, age three to five years. These outcomes, while more detailed, still tie directly to the six general skills of ECRR®.

Additional information on the ELGs specific to one state can generally be referenced by visiting the Early Learning tab of a state's Department of Education website.

Former United States Secretary of Education Richard W. Riley has said, "If every child were read to daily from infancy, it would revolutionize education in this country." Parents have that potential. Parents have the tremendous power to revolutionize their child's school experience and ultimate successes.

The balance of this book will look at the best practices for harnessing that power. The suggestions in the remaining chapters are based on both brain research and ECRR® 1 and 2 for exposing our littlest learners to a world of words through talking, reading, playing, singing, and interacting with our print-filled environment.

NOTES

1. M. Adams, *Beginning to Read: Thinking and Learning About Print* (Cambridge, MA: MIT Press, 1990).

2. C. Snow, M. Burns and P. Griffin, *Preventing Reading Difficulties in Young Children* (Washington DC: National Academy Press, 1998).

3. National Institute for Literacy, *Fast Facts on Literacy & Fact Sheet on Correctional Education* (Washington DC, 1998).

4. J. Kagan, N. Herschkowitz and E. Herschkowitz *A Young Mind in a Growing Brain* (Mahwah, NJ: Lawrence Erlbaum Associates, 2005).

5. C. Mangina and E. Sokolov, "Neuronal Plasticity in Memory and Learning Abilities: Theoretical Position and Selective Review," *International Journal of Psychophysiology* (2006): 203–214.

6. R. Nowakowski "Stable Neuron Numbers From Cradle to Grave," *Proceedings of the National Academy of Sciences of the United States of America* (2006): 12219–12220.

7. L. Fielding, "Kindergarten Learning Gap," *American School Board Journal* (April 2006): 32.

8. R. Arnold, "Public Libraries and Early Literacy: Raising a Reader," *American Libraries* (2003): 48–51.

9. "Every Child Ready to Read," last modified 2015, http://everychildreadytoread.org.

10. "Every Child Ready to Read, 2nd edition Manual," last modified 2015, http://everychildreadytoread.org.

11. "Trelease on Reading," last modified 2014, http://trelease-on-reading.com.

Chapter One

Talk Early and Talk Often

Before we are even aware it has happened, our babies' cries have turned into conversations. Parents who interact with their babies raise children who will succeed. Helping our babies acquire language is more natural than we think. Talking is one of the most natural things we do with the children in our care. When we talk about our day, sit down to snack and dinner, we help build important language skills through our conversations.

An infant acquires language when it is cared for in a positive environment that fosters trust and celebrates successes. Babies are prepared to speak from the time of birth. They use their cries, facial expressions, and body movements to communicate their wants and needs. Through nurturing and loving interactions, by the time a child is ten months of age, he has already learned how to recognize the speech sounds (or phonemes) of the language spoken by his caregivers. Through a responsive and repetitive process of talking and listening, the child has lost some of the capacity to distinguish and produce the phonemes of other languages.[1]

Babies all over the world babble in similar ways. Around the age of two, the sound of babble will begin to shape the sound of the child's native language. The word babble itself comes from the *ba-ba* sound babies make. Even in infancy babies are developing phonemic awareness as they repeat syllables and play with consonant sounds. Michael H. Goldstein, an assistant professor of psychology, has done experiments showing that babies learn language better from parental stimulation. That is, little ones best acquire new sounds and new sound patterns when their caregivers respond to their babble. When a baby is babbling, the baby is communicating to their parent that they are paying attention. When babbling, they are aroused and interested, and that is an optimal time to try a board book, sing a song, or play peekaboo.[2]

Photo 2.   Rhyming peekaboo games are a childhood favorite.

While speaking is a natural skill, reading and writing skills must be acquired. While human brains are naturally wired to speak, they are not naturally wired to read and write.[3] However, with instruction, children typically learn to read around age five or six. It requires another eight to sixteen years of schooling to master high-level reading comprehension.

The amount of talking parents do is directly related to a child's later language and reading development. A landmark study conducted in 1995 by Hart and Risley set out to understand why some children do better than others in school. Their experiment transcribed one hour of conversation between parents and their children in forty-two homes each month for three years. Their research concluded that there was a direct link between the academic success of a child and the number of words the child's parents spoke to the child before he/she turned three years old.[4] In a longitudinal follow-up of the children at ages nine and ten, the findings were persisting. The vocabulary levels of the children at age three were predictive of language test scores at ages nine and ten.

Talking to your child helps expand their vocabulary, develop their background knowledge, and inspire a curiosity about the world. It is through their social interactions that young children acquire the skills needed to maintain

Figure 1.1. The more parents talk to their children, the more their child's vocabulary grows.

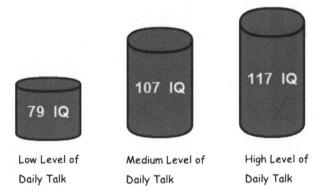

Figure 1.2. Children who come from homes rich in conversation have higher average IQ scores than children who live in quieter homes.

relationships. All of these skills developed in early childhood will eventually help that child learn to read! (Figures 1.1 and 1.2).

Research has shown that children learn new words by

- hearing a word repetitively,
- hearing words spoken by the important people in their lives, and
- hearing words in meaningful context.

The LENA Foundation set out to confirm and extend the research of Hart and Risley using new-found technology. As opposed to transcribing conversations like Hart and Risley, researchers for the LENA foundation relied on a kind of word pedometer to record the conversations of parents and children. They recorded conversations (or lack thereof) in 329 homes over a twelve-hour day for a minimum of six months. Follow-up home visits from the researchers and the use of LENAs in targeted families confirmed Hart and Risley's research. Both studies concluded that the number of words children hear relate to their academic performance.

The LENA group also reported the following:

- Parents self-report that they talk more to their children than they actually do.
- Mothers account for 75 percent of the talk in a child's development.
- Mothers talk about 9 percent more to daughters than sons.
- Parents talk more to their first-born children.
- Most adult talk with children is done in the late afternoon and early evening.
- Talkative children have talkative parents.
- The more a child watches television, the lower his language scores.
- Parents of autistic children talk less to children with more severe symptoms. If their child demonstrates gains in language skills, they talk more.
- When parents receive feedback on their language relationship with their child, they consistently increase the amount of talk they engage in.[5]

It is never too early to have back-and-forth chats with your baby. Talking to little ones introduces them to the world of voices, sounds, and words. From day one, babies are hearing information so they can later compute what they have heard and figure out how words and sentences fit together. These earliest parent-infant "talks" help babies learn how to communicate with others.

There is a real difference between talking that is a two-way conversation versus talking "at" a child whereby the caregiver talks and the child is expected to listen. This one-way talk is termed "business talk" and spoken out of necessity. "Stop squirming," "Lay down," and "Don't throw that" are examples of business talk.

Richer talk, that extra talk, involves more "back-and-forth" turns. This type of conversation builds on and connects with the child's statements, questions, and responses. These conversations help children learn how to use language and understand the meaning of new words. These extended conversations are spoken by choice.

When parents first begin these extended conversations, they may fear that they are just providing a running dialogue on what is happening. But with practice, the conversation expands to include the past and future. Optimally these conversations will involve different kinds of sentences like questions and statements. These conversations ideally include adjectives and adverbs that model descriptive language. Such extra talk is fun. It is descriptive, explanatory, and full of teachable moments.

Meredith Rowe, through her research at Harvard University, also confirmed Hart and Risley's discovery that parental talk of any kind is a good thing. She too demonstrated through her research that the number of words heard in infancy and toddlerhood is predictive of future vocabulary growth. Rowe continued and took her research a bit further and found that while the amount of words heard is a factor in predicting vocabulary growth, it is not the most significant indicator. The diversity of words is *more* predictive of future language skills.[6]

Rowe advises to move conversations beyond quantity and to consider quality. Her research demonstrated that from the ages of nine through eighteen months, complex words, interactive words, and words that tell stories, explain them, and make the babies imagine are important. Parents should be most concerned about talk that is extra (not business talk) as opposed to just talking a lot. With toddlers and preschoolers, using rare and sophisticated words are important. When children are experienced with talk about the past and future, their own syntax and narrative development improve. To implement quality talk, parents

- with infants should point and label a variety of objects.
- with toddlers should ask challenging questions and incorporate a diverse and sophisticated vocabulary.
- with toddlers and preschoolers should have conversations about past or future events.

An easy way to consistently increase the amount of talk with your baby is to have back-and-forth chats with your child. These chats help babies learn how to communicate with others. When starting on these chats, first let your baby see your lips and facial expressions. Make eye contact with your baby when you are talking to them. Slow down and be focused on your child. Get down to your child's level and respond.

In her book *30 Million Words: Building a Child's Brain* Dr. Dana Suskind summarizes her discoveries about language acquisition as a pediatric cochlear implant surgeon at the University of Chicago Medical School. Her research confirms that academic achievement begins on the first day of life. From the moment a new mother coos at her baby after delivery, she has started her newborn's road to language acquisition and school readiness. Dr. Suskind has developed an educational program for parents with the aim of guiding them toward a stronger parent–child language relationship. She has tested her program in and around Chicago and across demographic groups. Her 30 Million Words Initiative® advises parents to follow the three Ts:

- Tune in to what your child is doing;
- Talk more to your child using lots of descriptive words; and
- Take turns with your child as you engage in conversation.[7]

Interestingly, after concentrating on the three Ts, parents serve up more enriching words to their children. Just as the LENA Foundation suggested, when parents know what is best for their children, they will do that which is best.

How does a parent take the research and do what is best for their own child? (1) From day one, have daily conversations with your infant, let the baby see your lips and facial expressions. (2) Make eye contact with your baby when you are talking to them. (3) Slow down and be involved in that personal conversational exchange. (4) Get down to your child's level and respond to their grimaces, blinks, smiles, and utterances.

Consider your child's current familiarity with language when you are interacting with them. Experts in child development and education use the technical terms of "scaffolding" and the "Zone of Proximal Development." In simpler terms, as your child grows, your conversations with them should as well. Compromise between what your child already understands and what you can help him understand on a higher level. Your child can likely understand much more than what his own vocalizations indicate. When conversing with a receptive child, do the following:

- imitate—mimic the child's words and/or actions
- comment—react to the child's words and/or actions
- expand—take the child's word and/or actions and add a piece of new information
- question—ask about the child's words and/or actions
- answer—respond to the child's words and/or actions.

All of these response types require that the child use what they know and extend it a bit forward. It is certainly not necessary to use all of these response types in every conversation.

One way to talk to a newborn or an infant includes engaging in baby talk. Babies love to hear the voices of familiar people. They get excited, especially when they are spoken to in interesting ways. Talking to infants using a combination of both adult speech and "baby talk" can be especially interesting to little ones. Baby talk is sometimes called *Parentese* or *Motherese*. This is that type of speech where an adult talks to a child in an exaggerated slow and singsong way. For example, "Joey is sooooo sweet. Look at Joey, he is such a cuuuutie pie."

Parents naturally seem to shorten their sentences, lengthen their vowel sounds, and include longer pauses when they engage in parentese. When babies hear parentese, they are likely to look at you and make coos and babbles.

Babble is your baby's first attempt to communicate with you. As you attend to the sounds your baby makes, allow them time to respond back to you with more babbling. Nod your head and be patient with your baby. Encourage their vocalization to continue by adding, "Yes, mm-hmmm. Tell me more."

Language is quickly filling your child's brain, but all babies acquire language in their own time frame. A typical progression for most children follows the general pattern as illustrated in figure 1.3. While children's speech and language development follows a typical pattern, every child is different. If you have concerns about your child, never hesitate to consult your child's pediatrician.

	Hearing & Understanding	Talking
Birth to 3 months	• Startles at loud sounds • Quiets or smiles when spoken to • Seems to recognize your voice • Increases or decreases sucking behavior in response to sound	• Makes pleasure sounds (coo, goo) • Cries differently for different needs • Smiles when seeing you
4 to 6 months	• Moves eyes in direction of sound • Responds to changes of tone of voice • Notices toys that make sounds • Pays attention to music	• Babbling sounds more speech like, including sounds of *b, p* and *m* • Chuckles and laughs • Vocalizes pleasure and displeasure • Makes gurgling sounds during play
7 months to 1 year	• Turns and looks in the direction of sounds • Listens when spoken to • Recognizes words for common items (cup, book, shoe, juice) • Begins to respond to requests (Come here. Want more?)	• Babbling has long and short groups of sounds (tata upup) • Uses speech (non-crying) to get and keep attention • Uses gestures to communicate (waving, holding up arms to get picked up) • Imitates different speech sounds • Has one or two words by first birthday, may be unclear (mama, dada, dog, hi)

Figure 1.3. Typical Speech and Language Development. From: American Speech-Language-Hearing Association, 2016. http://www.asha.org/public/speech/development.

1 to 2 years	• Follows simple commands and understands simple questions (Roll the ball, Where is the dog?) • Listens to simple stories, songs and rhymes • Points to pictures in a book when name	• Says more words every month • Uses some one or two word questions (Where's daddy? Go bye-bye?) • Puts two words together (more milk, no tub)
2 to 3 years	• Understands some opposites (go-stop, yes-no, up-down) • Follows two step requests (Get your cup and bring it to me) • Listens to and enjoys hearing stories for longer periods of time	• Uses two or three words to talk about and ask for things • Uses k, g, f, t, d and n sounds • Speech is understandable by caregivers most of the time • Asks for objects by name • Asks why? • May stutter on some words or sounds
3 to 4 years	• Hears when called for from another room • Understands words for some colors (red, blue, green) • Understands words for some shapes (circle, square) • Understands words for family relationships (brother, aunt, grandmother)	• Uses 4 sentences at a time to talk about day • People outside of family understand speech • Answers who? what? and where? • Asks when? and how? • Says rhyming words (hat-cat) • Uses pronouns (I, you, me, we, they) • Uses some plurals (toys, birds, cars) • Sentences have more than 4 words. • Talks without repeating words or syllables
4 to 5 years	• Understands words for order (first, next, last) • Understands words for time (yesterday, today, tomorrow) • Follows multi-step directions • Understands most of what is said	• May make mistakes on l,s,r,v,z,ch,sh,th sounds • Names letters and numbers • Uses sentences that have more than one verb • Tells a short story • Can hold a conversation • Adjusts talk depending on audience (louder outside than inside, shortens sentences with a younger child1

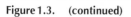

Figure 1.3.　　(continued)

Examples of Ways to Extend Baby's Babbles

- "Really? Then what happened? Tell me all about it."
- "Oh, I see. You have quite a story to tell today."
- "Yes, that's right. You are so smart Mary!"

SELF AND PARALLEL TALK

"Self talk" or a play-by-play type of conversation exposes children to thousands of words an hour. Don't be afraid to ramble with your little one. Imagine you are a radio or television broadcaster and your little one is your biggest fan. Use short sentences to talk about what you are seeing, hearing, or doing. "Parallel talk" is another way of narration where you describe what your child is seeing, hearing, and doing. Now you are like a sportscaster describing your baby's every action. Narrating is easy to do once you get started. Talk while performing daily routines like diapering, feeding, and playing. Describe what you are seeing as you pass objects. Be considerate to take some pauses from your narration to allow your child a chance to process all that you have said.

Examples of Self Talk

- "Clean up, clean up, a job that we can share. I'm picking up your clothes and toys. I have to pick up everywhere."
- "I'm pouring your milk. The milk is going into your blue cup."
- "I smell a stinky. It's time to change you."
- "Wash, wash, wash your hair (or hands, or belly, or bum). I wash it every day. I use some soap and a washcloth too. Let's wash those germs away."

Examples of Parallel Talk

- "Becky has found her toes. She is wiggling, wiggling, wiggling."
- "Yum-yum-yummy. Joey is so thirsty. Joey loves his bottle doesn't he?"
- "It's a sunny day. I bet you see the sunlight coming into the window."

IDENTIFICATION

When you are talking with your child, name things and take turns filling in the words when it is appropriate. Consider using some rhymes in your talk. Deliberately pause where that rhyming word should go; children are likely to be processing the word that you think belongs.

Examples of Identifying Things

- "Goodbye crib, goodbye room, goodbye house, goodbye driveway."
- "Here are Mary's fingers. Here are Mary's toes. Here is Mary's belly button, round and round it (_____) goes."
- "We're riding in our car. We're riding in our car. High-ho the dairy-o, we're riding in our car."
- "Your name is Baby. Baby starts with B. Bottle starts with B. Breakfast and banana start with B too. Do you hear all those bbbb sounds?"
- "What should you wear? How about a hat? You look good in (_____) that? How about a shoe? This shoe is (_____) new? Where's your coat? It makes you look like you can (_____) float."

ABSTRACT CONCEPTS

Talk about feelings and create an environment where language is in constant use. Children will learn that there are words to communicate almost anything.

Examples of Talking about Feelings

- "You're laughing Joey. Did you like that? Should we do that again?"
- "Mary is crying. Why are you crying, Mary? Are you hungry? Do you need a nap? Do you want me to hold you? I am sad when Mary is crying."
- "You heard Daddy, didn't you? You heard me coming to get you from your crib. I'm gonna get you!"

FUTURE TALK

Children easily add vocabulary that they can relate to their experiences. Giving them the words in advance will help solidify those word meanings in their minds.

Examples of Talking about What to Expect

- "It's thundering today. I hear thunder. I hear thunder. Loud, loud, thunder. Loud, loud thunder. Ssshhhhh. Now, I hear pitter-patter raindrops, pitter-patter raindrops. Soft, soft, rain. Soft, soft rain."
- "Mommy's taking Baby to the zoo tomorrow, the zoo tomorrow, the zoo tomorrow. Mommy's taking Baby to the zoo tomorrow and we can stay all day."

- The zoo is full of interesting animals I am going to carry Baby in her sling like a marsupial. Koalas and kangaroos are marsupials with pockets to carry their babies. We will have to find them when we visit tomorrow."
- "Grandma and Grandpa are here. Ding-dong-ding. Ding-dong-ding. I hear the doorbell ring. We hear that ding-dong song at church. We will hear the church bells chime before services this weekend."
- "Are we getting ready to go bye-bye? We are going to the store. What should we get? Mommy is consulting the sale advertisement and writing her grocery list now."

MATH TALK

Math is all around us. Just as the size of a child's vocabulary helps them learn to read, toddlers and preschoolers with a foundation in math vocabulary will become better math learners. Use math words in everyday conversations. Patterns, something that repeats more than once, help children make sense of math. Understanding patterns also aids in a child's ability to predict. The mathematical ideas of greater, less than, counting, measuring, estimating, and comparing are also ideas that take root in early childhood. Describe shapes and objects. Young children have a natural ability to understand shapes and mathematical ideas, so talk it up!

Examples of Talking With Math Concepts

- "What numbers do you see on that building? Our address and the numbers 1-2-3 as well."
- "Let's think, how many traffic lights have we passed? We've passed one, two, three, four traffic lights. How many more do you think we will see? You guess and we will keep count as we go to the park."
- "How many wheels do you see on our car? Does that big rig have more or less wheels than our car? What about daddy's motorcycle? Which kind of vehicle has the most wheels?"
- "How many pairs of socks are in the laundry basket? How many socks are in three pairs?"
- "Will you help me line up the fruits for our fruit salad from smallest to largest?"
- "How many sides does the cereal box have? Are they all the same shape?"
- "Can you find circles on that billboard?"
- "Look at the stripes on your shirt. They follow a pattern. What should come next? Red, blue, blue, red, blue, blue?"

STORYTELLING

Storytelling is just as valuable an experience to your child as reading a book. For young children, attending to an oral story offers the added dimension of imagination. They must visualize what the pictures in a book would do.

There is opportunity to share not only classic folk or fairy stories but stories from your own personal and family history. These are the stories that your child will treasure for the rest of her life.

Stories told orally offer the following advantages:

- Through repetitive phrases (and gestures), children develop vocabulary by joining in the story. A few examples from classic tales are:
  - "Little pig, little pig, let me come in. Not by the hair on my chinny chin." (*The Three little Pigs*)
  - "Run, run, as fast as you can. You can't catch me I'm the gingerbread man." (*The Gingerbread Man*)
  - "Fee-Fi-Fo-Fum. I smell the blood of an Englishman. Be he alive or be he dead. I'll grind his bones to make my bread." (*Jack and the Beanstalk*)
- Children can become physically involved through gestures and actions. Physical actions during a story encourages gross motor development.
  - "The little man seated himself in front of the wheel, and whirr, whirr, whirr, three turns, and the reel was full, then he put another on, and whirr, whirr, whirr, three times around, and the second was full too. And so it went on until the morning, when all the straw was spun, and all the reels were full of gold." (*Rumpelstiltskin*)
  - "At midnight in came two little elves; and they sat themselves on the shoemaker's bench. They took up all the leather that was cut out, and began to work with their little fingers, stitching and rapping and tapping away with little hammers so quickly that the shoemaker could not take his eyes off them." (*The Elves and the Shoemaker*)
- Storytellers make eye contact with their audience, allowing the story to take on a more personal tone. Children develop listening skills as well as the turn taking in verbal exchanges when they observe oral storytellers.

  - "Someone's been eating my porridge," growled the Papa bear.
    "Someone's been eating my porridge," said the Mama bear.
    "Someone's been eating my porridge and they ate it all up!"
        cried the Baby bear.
    (*Goldilocks and the Three Bears*)
  - "Grandmother, what big arms you have!"
    "All the better to hug you with, my dear."
    "Grandmother, what big legs you have!"

"All the better to run with, my child."
"Grandmother, what big ears you have!"
"All the better to hear you with, my child."
"Grandmother, what big eyes you have!"
"All the better to see you with, my child."
"Grandmother, what big teeth you have!"
"All the better to eat you up."
(*Little Red Riding Hood*)

NURSERY RHYMES AND MUSIC

Sharing music and rhyme with children is another way to spark the neurons in your youngster's brain. Young children enjoy the social experience of chanting, singing, and musical activities. But music is more than just enjoyable for young children. Lullabies have long helped babies sooth themselves. Music evokes feelings and teaches children to discriminate moods such as happiness, sadness, or fearfulness. Music styles from different cultures or heritages help children learn to respect those that are different from themselves.

Most toddlers naturally begin to dance when they hear music. In addition to exposing children to language, music offers the opportunity to foster gross motor skills. Children who are dancing need to stay balanced. Fingerplays and nursery rhymes support the development of small muscles and fine motor skills in little one's fingers.

- One, two, three, four, five, (hold up fingers one by one)
  Once I caught a fish alive. (put hands together and wiggle like a fish)
  Six, seven, eight, nine, ten, (hold up fingers one by one)
  Then I let him go again. (make throwing motion)
  Why did you let him go? (hold hands out asking why)
  Because he bit my finger so. (shake hand, as if hurt)
  Which finger did he bite? (hold hands out asking which)
  This little finger on my right. (wiggle pinky finger)
- Two little blackbirds sitting on a hill (hold up two fingers)
  One named Jack, (hold one finger out)
  One named Jill. (hold the other finger out)
  Fly away, Jack. (put one finger behind back)
  Fly away, Jill. (put the other finger behind back)
  Come back, Jack. (bring first finger back out front)
  Come back, Jill. (bring other finger back out front)
- Where is Thumbkin? (put both hands behind back)
  Where is Thumbkin?
  Here I am. (bring one thumb out front)
  Here I am. (bring the other thumb out front)

How are you today sir? (bend one thumb as if talking to the other)
Very well I thank you. (bend other thumb as if talking back)
Run away. (return first thumb behind back)
Run away. (return other thumb behind back)
Repeat with: Pointer, Tall Man, Ring Man, Small Man

It is through songs and nursery rhymes that children begin to hear the smallest parts of speech. Each beat of a song or rhyme often correlates to an individual syllable of a word. When children begin to read and write, the ability to break down words is vital. Most new readers hear the phrase "sound it out" repeatedly. The more songs and rhymes little ones are exposed to in the earliest of years, the easier it will be for them to sound out words in the future.

Some songs and rhymes for young children have been passed down for generations. They are fun, enjoyable, and provide for the development of a cozy relationship between caregiver and child. What we may forget as we pass on these seemingly outdated rhymes is that they are a first educational tool. Experts in early literacy have discovered that children who can recite eight nursery rhymes from memory by age four are likely to be among the best readers at age eight.[8]

Additionally,

- The sounds of vowels and consonants are clearly heard in nursery rhymes.
- The reciting of nursery rhymes allows children to play with pitch, volume, voice inflection, and the rhythm of language.
- Children hear rare words in nursery rhymes. For example, "Jack and Jill went up the hill to *fetch* a pail of water."
- Nursery rhymes are short and repetitive, mirroring children's own first sentences and attention spans.
- Nursery rhymes follow patterns that help children learn how to recall and memorize.
- Nursery rhymes often use numbers, counting, and math words.
- Mouth and tongue muscles are developed through rhyme.
- Rhymes with movement develop coordination.
- Children learn to imagine and then to dramatize rhymes.
- Clapping and rhyming with a caregiver establishes a positive association to language.
- Nursery rhymes teach history.
- Nursery rhymes are full of abstract concepts like emotion and humor.

While nursery rhymes appear to be fading from our vernacular, nursery rhymes and lap jogs are not only good for a child's growing vocabulary but are also fun lap activities to fill a parent's time interacting with the baby. Moving and bouncing with the baby is a great way to stay healthy and active together. Appendix A shares a wealth of these rhymes to enjoy together.

Children's Songs

Much of the music recorded for children is also intended to help them learn vocabulary and important concepts. Music can help them learn about their bodies like in, "Head, Shoulders, Knees and Toes." Children's songs introduce numbers and counting. Songs are repetitive and demonstrate the idea of patterning, which is a critical math skill. "Old Macdonald" is a song that allows children to predict and anticipate what comes next. Other songs, like "Froggy Went a Courtin'," tell a story that requires listening skills. Still others follow the sequence of beginning, middle, and end like in "The Farmer in the Dell." Such sequencing helps children learn story structure and narrative skills.

Young children benefit from appropriate music on a daily basis to stimulate brain activity.

Children who are able to keep a tempo and clap out a steady beat demonstrate higher achievement scores in first and second grades.[9] Luckily, chanting nursery rhymes, singing songs, and dancing are enjoyable activities for children. There is a wealth of children's rhymes and songs recorded each and every year. Music recording studios and artists know that singing and rhyming with children is an exceptional way to unknowingly teach young ones so many important early literacy skills.

Adults should never feel worried about their own singing voice or musical abilities. Children are not focused on musical ability. They are thrilled to be sharing a fun experience. Sharing music with little ones does not require a complicated performance. Instead, think of music as another way to have a conversation with your child.

As children grow, you may add marching, motions, and instruments to make the experience more enjoyable. As you share music with your child, look for ways to connect music to learning. Given below are some suggestions:

- Repeat the rhyming words and encourage your child to do the same.
- Discuss different types of music and find out your child's preference.
- Listen for details and ask your child if they hear different sounds, instruments, or new words.
- Introduce music vocabulary like lyric, note, and rhythm.
- Listen for any new words in song lyrics and define them if your child inquires.

Appendix B offers suggestions for a variety of music recorded specifically for children. These suggestions should keep you and your child moving, bouncing, and learning while staying healthy and active together.

INFANT SIGN LANGUAGE

Before infants can learn to talk, they may learn to use gestures to let you know what they want. If you wish, teach your child a few signs to ask for things or to tell you what she wants. This practice uses simple sign language to help a young child communicate with and talk to others. Signing can be a first step in making your child a communicator. The best signs are ones that can be used to ask for "more" or to say "yes" or "no." The first signs infants often learn are those for eat, drink, more, up, down, yes, and no. The chart below offers some of the easiest-to-learn signs (figure 1.4). If you are interested in sign language, there are many resources available on the internet for more information.

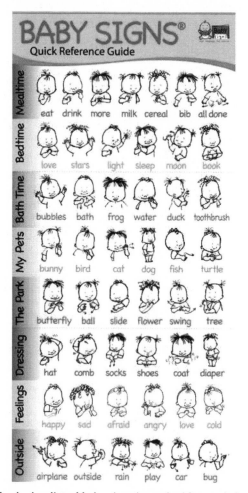

Figure 1.4. This beginning list of baby signs is used with permission from Baby Signs Too. Visit the website at www.babysignstoo.com/ for more information.

A THOUGHT ON TECHNOLOGY

The American Academy of Pediatrics and Dr. Dana Suskind in her 30 Million Words Initiative® agree on another parenting practice that is a challenge in our technological world.

Pediatricians recommend no screen time before a child reaches the age of two. Adding to her program of three "Ts," Dr. Suskind adds a fourth "T."

Turn it off.

When a young child is in front of a screen, the other three "Ts" are impossible. When a little one is involved in technology, they are NOT taking turns in conversations.

Turn off the television and unplug devices. Even the most educational of offerings are not a substitute for one-on-one and face-to-face interactions. If television is a necessity, turn on the closed captioning for your child. If nothing else, the child will be seeing the symbols of our language and relate them to the words being said. This is by no account a substitution for holding a conversation or reading a story book in your lap. But, if a busy caregiver needs time to make dinner or shower, the closed captioning puts written words in the minds of children.

Talking to babies and toddlers is a gift we offer our children. It is a gift that enriches brain development, improves the ability to learn, and reinforces the power of language. Use language as an accompaniment to play, to routine chores such as diapering, and to daily living experiences. Be proud of the priceless "brain power" you are giving your child. When it comes to brain building, the silence from "pre-baby" is totally overrated.

NOTES

1. P.K. Kuhl, K.A. Williams, F. Lacerda, K.N. Stevens, and B. Lindblom, "Linguistic Experience Alters Phonetic Perception in Infants by 6 Months of Age," *Science* (1992): 606–608.

2. M. Goldstein, "Social Feedback to Infants' Babbling Facilitates Rapid Phonological Learning," *Psychological Science* (May 2008) 19: 515–523.

3. I.Y. Liberman, D. Shankweiler, and A.M. Liberman, "The Alphabetic Principle and Learning to Read," Haskin Laboratories Status Report on Speech Research (1990).

4. B. Hart and T.R. Risley. *Meaningful Differences in the Everyday Experiences of Young American Children* (Baltimore, MD: Paul H. Brookes, 1995).

5. J. Gilkerson and J. Richards. "The Power of Talk, 2nd edition," The LENA Foundation (2009).

6. M.L. Rowe, K.A. Leech, and N. Cabrera, "Going Beyond Input Quantity: Wh-Questions Matter for Toddlers' Language and Cognitive Development," *Cognitive Science* (2016): 162–179.

7. D. Suskind. *Thirty-Million Words: Building a Child's Brain* (New York: Dutton, 2015).

8. M. Fox, *Reading Magic* (San Diego, CA: Harcourt, 2001).

9. P.S. Weikart, L.J. Schweinhart, and M. Larner, "Movement Curriculum Improves Children's Rhythmic Competence," *HighScope ReSource* (1987): 8–10.

Chapter Two

Bring on the Books

In 1983, the United States Department of Education summoned its first Commission on Reading to investigate a perceived decline in reading activities by the American public. In *"Becoming a Nation of Readers,"* the conclusion "The single most important activity for building the knowledge required for eventual success in reading is reading aloud to children"[1] was drawn. As we discuss emerging literacy, it is critical to explore how best to share books with young children. The three most predictive factors to kindergarten reading achievement are the following:

- access to high-quality books
- book ownership
- child's experience in book selection.

Read books often! Talk about them, sing them, play with them, and yes, read them! Allow your child to talk about the books, sing about them, play with them, and they can read them again. When you are both through, do it all over again! Hearing the words in books, even if they are the same words repetitively, fuels neural building that is going on in the child's supple brain.

When it comes to building rich vocabulary, children's picture books are our best tool. When studying our vocabulary patterns, researchers have determined that there are ten thousand different words that we use in our daily activities. These words are termed as "common" words. All other words are referred to as "rare" words. While rare words are not typically used in conversation, we must be familiar with these words to understand the complex and abstract ideas in print. Generally speaking, children's picture books have thirty-one rare words per thousand. In comparison, our daily conversation with our children (six months to ten years of age) contains twelve rare words per thousand. Statistically, a good children's book is three times richer in rare vocabulary words than conversation. Those "rare" words create richer and thicker brain connections. The more "rare" (or book) words a child knows, the more easily he will be able to read and comprehend complex ideas. It is impossible to read and comprehend words we have never heard before.

Knowing that neural connections between brain cells are strengthened through repetition, teachers, librarians, and other caring adults advocate "Read every day." They know that these three words, in practice, will change the outcome of a life. The general guideline is that the parents spend at least fifteen minutes a day reading to their children. Those fifteen minutes may be in small segments for young kiddos or all in one sitting for older children. Preschoolers might listen to a chapter book for the entire reading session or prefer several picture books. Reading for a longer period of time is never discouraged. In busy families reading to young children may become burdensome to some caregivers, especially when there are multiple children of differing ages. Children should never feel that reading is a chore. Given below are suggestions for helping parents achieve their minimum goal of reading every day for fifteen minutes:

- Make reading part of a daily routine during breakfast, perhaps after bath or before bed.
- Read one title out loud to all children and schedule an individual reading "date" that alternates among the children.
- Take reading field trips whereby you read in a park, at the library, in a restaurant, or at the playground.

Begin reading to your child in infancy. At first your baby is simply enjoying the sound of your voice and finds the rhythm soothing. During these encounters your child is establishing a positive relationship with books. They are connecting your familiar and pleasant voice to books, and they are learning that reading gives pleasure.[2] Human beings are pleasure centered. When something sends a pleasure message to our brain, we want to revisit that experience. When a child experiences pleasures while reading, their instinct is to continue to search out that reading opportunity.

During infancy it is appropriate to spend five- to ten-minute intervals reading out loud to your baby when they are receptive. Don't worry if the baby is more interested in chewing the book or using it as a play thing. Through these trials children develop book knowledge. They learn that books open, close, and look awkward when they are turned upside down. Some experts believe that parents who treat reading as entertainment as opposed to a skill ultimately develop children who have a more positive attitude toward reading.[3] Infancy is the time to start entertaining with books.

The time you spend reading to your child can lengthen as your child ages. By toddlerhood, young children can spend twenty-minute intervals listening to several stories. While they may wiggle and wander, they are still hearing those critical words. Be cautious not to force a child to stay in your lap or listen to books when they are clearly uncooperative. The opposite effect is valid: children with early negative book experiences will develop a poor attitude toward reading. Reading or listening to a story should never be used as a punishment or a reward that can be bargained away. Those consequences create an idea that books hold less value and can be squandered.

By preschool, children have the attention span to listen to longer books and for longer periods of time. From board books to picture books, reading material should grow along with your child. In addition to being a perfect way to engage your child in the six early literacy skills needed to become an independent reader, book sharing is beneficial for additional reasons. They are as follows:

- Children improve their listening skills when they listen to a story.
- Children develop longer attention spans from listening to stories read aloud.
- Children are introduced to new vocabulary during book sharing.
- Children hear more uncommon words from picture books than adult conversation or television viewing.[4]

As you read, children are watching the pages turn and the text flow from left to right, and they learn that illustrations correspond to written words. This preliteracy skill called "print awareness" or book-handling behavior is not something that is ever explicitly taught to children. It is a skill that is acquired through shared reading experiences. Children with a sense of print awareness become the best readers in kindergarten.[5]

Listening to stories stimulates a child's imagination. Children imagine what the character of a book is experiencing. Through their imaginations and their experiences, they can experience things that are impossible in their own small world.

As children follow a character through a story, they develop empathy for others. For example, in the classic "*Where the Wild Things Are*" by Maurice Sendak, children feel sorry for Max when he is sent to bed hungry. Then, when Max ends his wild rumpus and returns home, children can feel the relief of a homecoming. Children who have experienced the same relief of "coming home" are reassured that their feelings are not unusual and are valid.

The more pleasant read-aloud experiences a child has, the more they enjoy reading. The more they enjoy reading, the more they will love books. The more they love books, the more they will want to read. Once a child can read, there is no limit to what they can learn. This circular pattern of loving to read and learn is a priceless gift that will continue providing for your child well into adulthood.

Language is symbol oriented. When we read, we are converting symbols (letters) into words. In early childhood, children learn that those words represent some "thing" in our environment. When we have broken this code we are ready to read. The process by which we read is in fact called "decoding." For example, in the sentence "The boy ran into the sprinkler," our brains are converting the letters of b, o, and y into the sounds each letter makes. B, o, and y become /boi/. Instantaneously our brains assign /boi/ to the little human who lives in the next yard. Our brain processes all of this as quickly as the messages cross from one neuron to the next.

The stronger the neural foundation in our brains, the quicker the conversion from sounds to meaning can occur. Our brain must decode every word we hear, read, and speak. In the above example, if we rearrange some of the words to "The boy sprinkled," our coding for the words stays the same, but the pieces are rearranged. This part of reading is called "comprehending." Children must quickly decode and comprehend what they see in text. As we read to our children, their brain is processing all of the possible code combinations.

The more experience children have with stories and words, the better they become at cracking the code of language. The children who do not have sufficient decoding skills in early childhood are unlikely to overcome the deficit. Ninety percent of the poor readers in first grade have failed to master the decoding process. These struggling children continue to battle with reading throughout their academic career. While our brains are naturally wired to speak, the code-breaking of the reading and writing process needs to be practiced and perfected.

Reading out loud to young children cannot be excessive. Every story they hear helps their brain become a little quicker at making the necessary connections needed for the complex process of reading. We know that a mere delay in decoding word one of a sentence results in another delay in decoding word two of the sentence. The ultimate delay lengthens across the sentence. While that child is struggling in sentence one, in that split second of difference, the teacher and more successful classmates have proceeded to sentence two.

Babies may appear utterly uninterested and passive when we first begin reading to them. But their active brains are busy creating connections and storing information about our language code. Babies' brains are physically growing in response to all this language they are hearing. By the age of three a child's brain has grown from 25 percent of adult capacity at birth to 85 percent of adult capacity at age three. A baby's brain is also twice as active as an adult's. Feeding that growing brain with the nourishing words from books is critical.

These early years are considered prime time for brain and language development. Studies confirm that the number of books physically in a home directly predicts reading achievement. On the converse, a lack of book nourishment during a child's initial years has profound negative effects on that child's academic future. Establish a regular reading time during the tender years of early childhood. When you create a habit of reading, it will remain a special activity for you and your child.

READING WITH YOUR BABY, ZERO TO TWELVE MONTHS

A loving bond is created when you hold your baby and read to them. Your familiar voice and reassuring touch has a calming effect on your little one and creates the association that reading is a pleasurable activity. Parent of infants may question how to share a book with an infant who isn't yet strong enough to hold up their own head. We know that children at this age understand more than they indicate. Their "coos" may be their response to hearing you read. When reading to your infant, the following tips may prove helpful:

- Hold your baby on your lap while you read. Let your baby explore soft cloth, vinyl, or board books.
- Babies learn by exploring with their mouth, and some baby books should be "chewable."
- Point at pictures and name them as you turn the pages. If your baby is willing, use their little fingers to follow along as you point out pictures and words.
- Ask your baby questions about what is happening on the page, such as, "Where is the puppy?" Pause, point, and allow time for the baby to process your question. Then continue, "Oh, we found it, there's the puppy!"
- In the first few months, the baby's eye sight is still developing and holding the books about 10 inches away from your child is optimal.
- When reading to a baby, following the printed text of the author is optional. You don't need to read the words as they appear; talk about the pictures with baby. The reader is allowed to create their own story as they explore the pictures with baby.
- Be sensitive to the baby's mood. If yourr baby is fussy or uncomfortable, stop reading and start again at another time. Forcing a reluctant baby to take part in a read-aloud session is counterproductive to the goal of creating positive book experiences.
- It is okay if your baby crawls or moves away; the baby is still hearing the words and benefiting from your book-sharing time. Continue reading.

- The public library has free story times for children of all ages starting at birth. Young infants are intrigued by hearing another voice read to them. Often playgroups sprout from these infant story times. Seek out these opportunities and make them part of your routine.
- Start a tradition of gifting books on special occasions. Adding inscriptions help document your child's growth and often become cherished heirlooms.

Twenty Favorite Titles to Share with Your Baby

Alborough, Jez. *Hug*. Cambridge, MA: Candlewick Press, 2000.

Baker Keith. *Big Fat Hen*. San Diego, CA: Harcourt Brace, 1994.

Boynton, Sandra. *Belly Button Book*. New York: Workman Publishing Company, 2005.

——. *Tickle Time!* New York: Workman Publishing Company, 2012.

Brown, Margaret Wise. *Goodnight Moon*. New York: Harper & Row, 1947.

Cabrera, Jane. *Ten in the Bed*. New York: Holiday House, 2006.

Carle, Eric. *The Very Hungry Caterpillar*. New York: Philomel Books, 1987.

Church, Caroline Jayne. *Ten Tiny Toes*. New York: Cartwheel Books, 2014.

Dunrea, Olivier. *Gossie*. Boston, MA: Houghton Mifflin Company, 2002.

Fleming, Denise. *Barnyard Banter*. New York: Holt, 1994.

Hill, Eric. *Where's Spot*. New York: Putnam, 1980.

Katz, Karen. *Zoom, Zoom, Baby*. New York: Little Simon, 2014.

McBratney, Sam. *Guess How Much I Love You*. Somerville, MA: Candlewick Press, 1994.

Miller, Margaret. *What's On My Head?* New York: Little Simon, 2009.

Opie, Iona. *Snuggle Up With Mother Goose*. Somerville, MA: Candlewick Press, 2015.

Raffi. *Down By The Bay*. *New York: Crown Publishers, 1987.*

Rossetti-Shustak, Bernadette. *I Love You Through and Through*. New York: Cartwheel Books, 2005.

Siomades, Lorianne. *Itsy Bitsy Spider*. Honesdale, PA: Boys Mills Press, 1999.

Watt, Fiona. *That's Not My Series (Usborne Touchy-Feely Books.)* Osborne Books Limited, 2002–2010.

Wood, Don. *Piggies*. San Diego, CA : Harcourt Brace Jovanovich, 1991.

Figure 2.1.

Babies like . . .

- board books, vinyl books, cloth books, and textured books they can touch and feel
- small books that fit into their hands
- books with bold, clear pictures of objects found in the baby's world
- pictures of other babies, especially faces
- books that can be sung or books that rhyme
- books with rhythm and repetition
- books with animal sounds
- the same book, repetitively.

READING WITH YOUR YOUNG TODDLER, TWELVE TO TWENTY-FOUR MONTHS

Toddlers, like their own rapidly developing brains, are forever in motion. As they begin to speak, you may recognize their first words are those from their favorite books. Toddlers have short attention spans, so reading times may need to be quick in duration but occur more frequently.

Toddlers rarely give a book their undivided attention. Even in motion, your toddler is listening. Try "skipping" a favorite book passage; your toddler is likely to protest. As toddlers gain verbal skills, they may be able to fill in a word you have purposely left out of a story or rhyme. Allow your toddler to catch your mistakes and reward their keen observation skills. "You're right, the bird did find its mommy." Allow your child to interact with the book. Allow them to interrupt and ask questions. Allow them to find and comment on the pictures. Interacting with the stories in such ways is evidence that your toddler's brain is hard at work. Conversation, touching, and pointing during a reading session is success. Some additional tips for sharing books with toddlers are as follows:

- Read every day and read often, even if it is only for a few minutes at a time.
- Have fun; reading should not be a chore!
- Talk about the pictures. Do not be tied to every word in a book. Lengthen or shorten the story based on your child's mood.
- Make up your own stories and relate them to your experiences.
- Let your child hold the book and turn the pages when they are capable and interested.

- Toddlers love to hear their names in stories. Try substituting their names into the books you share.
- Run your finger along the words as you read them.

Young toddlers like . . .

- sturdy board books they can handle, carry, stack, and use as building blocks
- books that show children sleeping, eating, and playing
- goodnight books for bedtime
- books about saying hello and goodbye
- books with only a few words on the page
- books with simple rhymes or predictable text.

READING WITH YOUR OLDER TODDLER, TWENTY-FOUR TO THIRTY-SIX MONTHS

The key to sharing books with the ever-in-motion toddler is to identify times during the day when she is most receptive. Trying to read to a toddler who wants to play outside or with newly discovered toys will frustrate both of you. Never force books on an unwilling child. Book sharing should never be a punishment.

Reading with older toddlers who are becoming verbal should be interactive. Encourage your child to join you in the repetition of familiar phrases in a book. For example, in the classic *"The Very Hungry Caterpillar"* by Eric Carle, your toddler can recite, "But he was still hungry." When reading with an older toddler consider the following:

- Read favorite stories again and again. The more a child hears a story, the more they are able to participate and stronger neural connections will be made.
- Read labels and signs wherever you go. As your toddler recognizes familiar logos and signs, commend their "reading" ability. McDonald's is often a first. Point out other "M"s as you see them. Using the signs around us will be discussed at greater length in chapter 5.
- Allow your child to choose their books. Keep books in different areas of your home. If your child is toilet training, a basket of books by the potty helps pass time. Try reading books about going to the potty for inspiration.
- Choose books about events that mirror your child's life: stories about starting preschool, visiting the doctor, traveling to grandma's house, or about a family pet will be enjoyed by your older toddler.
- Ask your child questions about the story, even if they cannot yet answer. "What do you think will happen next? What is this? Was that a good idea for Bear?" Provide answers to your questions if your child isn't willing.

- Create voices for the characters and make silly sounds for the animals when appropriate.

Photo 3. Reading is part of the bedroom routine for these siblings. This little guy causes toddler trouble just like the character in the story he is hearing.

Your child will enjoy making the animal sounds too. Animal sounds are common in books for this age group. Animal sounds are actually small phonemes (syllables) that will help the decoding and "sounding out" process they will use when they begin formal reading instruction.

Older toddlers like . . .

- to help turn the pages
- to fill in the words of a story they know
- to point and identify pictures
- to hear the same book over and over
- books that are silly
- books with pictures and names of many different things
- books with board pages and also "big kid" books with paper pages
- books with rhyme, rhythm, and repeated text
- books about children and families
- books about food, animals, trucks, dinosaurs, and other favorite subjects.

Twenty Favorite Titles to Share with Your Toddler

Barner, Bob. *Bugs, Bugs, Bugs*. San Francisco, CA: Chronicle Books, 1999.

Campball, Rod. *Dear Zoo: A Lift the Flap Book*. New York: Little Simon, 2007.

Carle, Eric. *From Head to Toe*. New York: HarperCollins, 1997.

Christelow, Eileen. *Five Little Monkeys Jumping on the Bed.* New York: Clarion Books, 1989.

Crews, Donald. *Freight Train*. New York: Greenwillow Books, 1978.

Dean, James. *Pete the Cat: I Love My White Shoes*. New York: Harper, 2010.

Dewdney, Anna. *Llama, Llama Red Pajama*. New York: Penguin Group USA, 2015.

Ehlert, Lois. *Planting a Rainbow*. San Diego, CA : Harcourt Brace Jovanovich, 1988.

Feiffer, Jules. *Bark George*. New York: HarperCollins Publishers, 1999.

Fleming, Denise. *Mama Cat Has Three Kittens*. New York: Henry Holt, 1998.

Foley, Greg E. *Don't Worry Bear*. New York: Viking, 2008.

Hall, Zoe. *The Surprise Garden*. New York: Blue Sky Press, 1998.

Henkes, Kevin. *Little White Rabbit*. New York: Greenwillow Books, 2011.

——*Kitten's First Full Moon*. New York: Greenwillow Books, 2004.

Katz, Karen. *Counting Kisses*. New York: Little Simon, 2010.

Martin Jr, Bill. *Chicka Chicka Boom Boom*. New York: Beach Lane Books, 2009.

——*Brown Bear, Brown Bear, What Do You See?* New York: Henry Holt, 1996.

Miller, Virginia. *Ten Red Apples*. Cambridge, MA: Candlewick Press, 2002.

Numeroff, Laura Joffe. *If You Give a Mouse a Cookie*. New York: HarperCollinsPublishers, 1985.

Savage, Stephen. *The Mixed-Up Truck*. New York: Roaring Brook Press, 2016.

Shannon, David. *No, David!* New York: Blue Sky Press, 1998.

Shaw, Charles Green. *It Looked Like Spilt Milk*. New York, NY: HarperCollins, 1947.

Stoeke, Janet Morgan. *A Hat for Minerva Louise*. New York: Dutton Children's Books, 1994.

Strickland, Paul. *Dinosaur Roar*. New York: *Puffin Books,* 1994.

Sullivan, Mary. *Ball.* New York: Houghton Mifflin Harcourt Publishing Company, 2016.

Tafuri, Nancy. *All Kinds of Kisses*. New York: LB Kids, 2014.

——*Blue Goose*. New York: Simon & Schuster Books for Young Readers, 2008.

Walsh, Ellen Stoll. *Mouse Paint*. San Diego, CA: Harcourt Brace Jovanovich, 1989.

Willems, Mo. *Don't Let the Pigeon Drive the Bus!* New York: Hyperion Books for Children, 2003.

Wood, Don. *The Little Mouse, the Red Ripe Strawberry and the Big Hungry Bear*. New   York: Child's Play (International), 1984.

Figure 2.2.

READING WITH YOUR PRESCHOOLER,
THREE TO FIVE YEARS

Preschool children are now interested in choosing some of their own books. Selecting a book is a part of early literacy. A preschooler is ready to discuss books with you. Allow time for your preschooler to ask questions about the story and answer them as best you can. This is a great time to ask your preschooler, "What do you think?" Don't be concerned that the reading has been interrupted. Encourage discussion by asking questions that require more than a yes or no answer. "What is in the picture?" "What do you think the mommy is doing now?" "How do you think the baby is feeling?" This important strategy, "Dialogic Reading," is important to implement with preschoolers. More about Dialogic Reading is shown in figure 2.3 below. Some questions that are useful in incorporating Dialogic Reading in both fiction and nonfiction stories are given in the figures 2.4 and 2.5.

When possible, supplement the book you are sharing with your preschooler with a hands-on experience. For example, after reading *Blueberries for Sal* by Robert McCloskey, go outside (or the grocery store) to pick berries and eat them over ice cream for dessert. While enjoying dessert, recall the story, construct a book-related craft, or take a field trip to further the story experience. After reading *Brown Bear, Brown Bear, What Do You See?* by Bill Martin Jr., visit the zoo and discuss the colors of the animals or be on the lookout for a zookeeper. The more a preschooler has personal and tangible experiences with a book, the deeper they will make brain connections.

Preschoolers love to read favorite books but are also curious about new books. Preschoolers also like to read nonfiction titles that will answer questions they have about their world. Now is the ideal time to introduce books that are true and answer all those "why" questions your child seems to be asking. Visit your local library often. Now is the perfect time to experiment with different types of books. Trying books and deciding you don't like them is a valuable experience.

This is an opportunity to discuss "Why don't you like this book?" "Does this remind you of another book we read?" or "How do you feel about the pictures?" Now is also a perfect time to get your child a library card of their very own. Children enjoy the ownership of having their own card and choosing books for themselves. Keep in mind that children can usually read on one level but can understand books that are written on a higher level. It is not until eighth grade that reading level and listening level are equal. When reading with your preschooler, consider the following:

- Use expression. Change your tone of voice to fit the dialogue.
- Adjust your reading pace to the story. If the story is exciting, read more quickly. If it is a suspenseful story, read more slowly.

Children learn most from books when they are actively involved in the reading experience. Researchers have developed a method of reading called *Dialogic Reading*. In dialogic reading, the adult helps the child become the teller of the story. The adult becomes the questioner and the audience for the child. By asking questions about the story, the adult is leading the child into conversation about the book.

This technique is effective with children who already have a beginning vocabulary of at least 50 expressive words. Toddlers, especially between the ages of 19 and 24 months, are developing a tremendous growth in vocabulary. Some researchers have suggested that this age group acquires about 9 new words every day. Dialogic Reading is a wonderful way to make the most of our toddler's "vocabulary-spurt."

The Three Steps of Dialogic Reading

1. Ask "what" questions. Ask your child, "What's this?" or "What's this called?" Repeat your child's response and acknowledge that their response is correct. "Yes Baby, that is a bird".

2. Expand on your child's answer. Keep the expansions short and simple so that your child is later able to imitate what you've said. For example, "Yes Baby, that is a bird! It's a yellow bird." Some days your child may be receptive to continuing that conversation, "What is the yellow bird doing?" "Yes, it does look like he is making a nest."

3. Ask open-ended questions. When your child is eager to answer all of your "what" questions, begin asking "open-ended" questions. Open-ended questions require more thought and the use of imagination. Open ended questions ask for opinions and do not have a correct answer. For example: "Why do you think that bird is building a nest?" Or, "Why do you think bird's live in nests?" If your child cannot answer your open-ended question, help them by answering the question yourself. "I wonder if the bird needs a nest because she has eggs to protect. Maybe that bird is going to become a mommy bird. What do you think?"

Not every page of a story requires dialogic reading. Likewise, every reading session need not be composed of dialogical reading. Sometimes a child just wants to listen to a story and snuggle in a caregiver's lap. Other days, your child may be more expressive and want to tell you about every picture. Follow your child's lead, praise their ideas and encourage the interesting conversations that reading will spark.

Figure 2.3.   Dialogic Reading is an important strategy to implement while reading out loud.

- Try wordless books and allow your child to "read" it to you. Commend their ability to "read" and tell a story.
- When your child has learned the first letter of her name, point out that letter in the titles of books you read.
- When your child has recognized a sight word, encourage them to point out that word when they see it in print.
- When you notice alliteration of a particular sound in a book, discuss it with your child and discuss which letter is responsible for making those repetitive sounds.
- When your child is interested, add audio books to your child's listening experiences. These choices should not replace the interactions you share

- Who is this story about? Do you know anyone like him/her?
- Did anyone have a problem in the story? What was the problem?
- How would you have resolved the problem?
- What else could the character have done to resolve the problem?
- Are you at all like the character? How?
- What do you think will happen next?
- Why do you think the author chose to _____?
- Can you think of a different title for this story?
- Would you like to be friends with anyone n the story? Who and why?
- What parts of this story could and could not really happen?
- Did you like the story? Why or why not?
- What was your favorite part of the story? Why?
- Does this story remind you of any other stories you have read or heard before? Which story?
- Did you like the pictures in the story?
- How would you draw the characters in the story?

- What did you learn from reading this?
- What did you already know about ___(subject)___?
- What is something new you know about (the subject) ?
- Is there anything else you wonder about ___(the subject)___?
- Why do you think the author wrote this?
- What would be a good title for this reading?
- Have you read any other books about ___(subject)___? Which did you enjoy more? Why?
- Did you have a favorite picture? Which one and why?
- Did you learn any new words from this reading?

Figure 2.4 and 2.5. **The questions you use to encourage dialogue may vary if the story is fiction or nonfiction.**

when you read books together, however. Technology does not allow for Dialogic Reading or book discussion.
- Include newspapers, magazines, encyclopedias, catalogs, recipes, atlases, sports programs, and advertisements throughout your day. Sharing your text and e-mail messages demonstrates that understanding print is a vital skill for survival in our print-filled world.

Preschoolers like . . .

- books that tell stories and have a clear beginning, middle, and end
- books about kids who look like and live like them
- books about different places and different ways of living
- books about going to school or day care
- books about making friends
- counting books, alphabet books, search and find books
- books about their interests and books they have chosen on their own
- stories of their caregivers, that they themselves have made up

In appendix C, you will find a list of hundred picture books (appropriate for children from birth through five) with which all incoming kindergarteners should be familiar. To get your reading started, below are list of books beloved by preschoolers.

Forty Titles to Share with Your Preschooler

Aylesworth, Jim. *Old Black Fly*. New York: Holt, 1992.

Bang, Molly. *When Sophie Gets Angry – Really, Really Angry*. New York: Blue Sky Press, 1999.

Beaumont, Karen. *I Ain't Gonna Paint No More!* Orlando, FL: Harcourt, 2005.

Bemelmans, Ludwig. *Madeline*. New York: Puffin Books, 1939.

Cronin, Doreen. *Click, Clack, Moo Cows That Type*. New York: Simon & Schuster Books for Young Readers, 2000.

Daywalt, Drew. *The Day The Crayons Quit*. New York: Philomel Books, 2013.

de la Peña, Matt. *Last Stop on Market Street*. New York: GP Putnam's Sons, 2015.

DiPucchio, Kelly. *Gilbert Goldfish Wants a Pet*. New York: Dial Books for Young Readers, 2011.

Eastman, P.D. *Are You My Mother?* New York: Random House Books For Young Readers, 1960.

Falconer, Ian. *Olivia*. New York: Atheneum Books for Young Readers, 2000.

Freedman, Claire. *Pirates Love Underpants*. New York: Aladdin, 2013.

Gaiman, Neil. *Chu's Day*. New York: Harper Collins Childrens, 2013.

George, Lindsay Barrett. *That Pup*. New York: Greenwillow, 2011.

Henkes, Kevin. *Chrysanthemum*. New York: Greenwillow Books, 1991.

—. *Lilly's Purple Plastic Purse*. New York: Greenwillow Books, 2006.

Heos, Bridget. *Mustache Baby*. New York: Clarion Books, 2013.

Hills, Tad. *Duck and Goose*. New York: Schwartz & Wade Books, 2006.

Hutchins, Hazel. *SNAP!* Toronto; New York; Vancouver: Annick Press, 2015.

Hutchins, Pat. *Good-Night, Owl!* New York: Macmillan, 1972.

Jeffers, Oliver. *The Heart and the Bottle*. New York: Philomel Books, 2010.

Kann, Victoria. *Pinkalicious*. New York: HarperCollins, 2006.

Keats, Ezra Jack. *Snowy Day*. New York: Puffin Books, 1962.

Figure 2.6.

Long, Melinda. *How I Became a Pirate*. San Diego, CA: Harcourt, 2003.

McMullen, Kate & Jim. *I Stink!* New York: Joanna Cotler Books, 2002.

McQuin, Anna. *Lola Plants a Garden*. Watertown, MA: Charlesbridge, 2014.

O'Connor, Jane. *Fancy Nancy*. New York: Harper, 2006.

Parsley, Elise. *If You Ever Want to Bring a Piano to the Beach, Don't!* New York: Little, Brown and Company, 2016.

Pfister, Marcus. *Rainbow Fish*. New York: North-South Books, 1992.

Ruzzier, Sergio. *Bear and Bee*. New York: Disney Hyperion Books, 2013.

Rylant, Cynthia. *The Great Gracie Chase: Stop That Dog*. New York: Blue Sky Press, 2001.

Sauer, Tammi. *I Love Cake!: Starring Rabbit, Porcupine, and Moose*. New York: Katherine Tegan Books, 2016.

Sendak, Maurice. *Where The Wild Things Are*. New York: HarperCollins,1963.

Shannon, David. *Duck on a Bike*. New York: Blue Sky Press, 2002.

Slobodkina, Sephyr. *Caps For Sale: A Tale of a Peddler, Some Monkeys and Their Monkey Business*. New York: HarperCollins, 1968.

Taback, Simms. *There Was an Old Lady Who Swallowed a Fly*. New York: Viking, 1997.

Teckentrup, Britta. *Get Out of My Bath*. Somerville, MA 2015

Underwood, Deborah. *Good Night, Baddies*. New York: Beach Lane Books, 2016.

Waddell. Martin. *Owl Babies*. Cambridge, MA: Candlewick Press, 1992.

Walsh, Melanie. *Monster, Monster*. Cambridge, MA: Candlewick Press, 2002.

Wiesner, David. *The Three Pigs*. New York: Clarion Books, 2001.

Willems, Mo. *Elephant & Piggie Books*. New York: Disney Hyperion, 2007-2016.

Wilson, Steve. *Hedgehugs*. New York: Henry Holt and Company, 2015.

Figure 2.6.

READING AND WRITING GO HAND IN HAND

Reading and writing are fundamental skills that will be used throughout a lifetime. The understanding of writing develops over time. Just like learning to read, the ability to decode (to convert marks on a page to the sounds they represent) must be learned. Children must also learn how to share the code and use it to convey their own thoughts and ideas. When a child scribbles, they are showing adults that they understand that the marks on pages mean something.

At around eighteen months, children will try to include letters and shapes into their scribbles. They may also show breaks between their scribbles representing an understanding that letters construct words and words construct sentences. When your toddler is drawing or scribbling, you can talk about their activity. Ask about the colors they are using. Identify shapes and letters you see in their creation. Ask them to tell you what is happening in the picture. Even without writing text, drawing time is a superb opportunity to share a conversation.

Children develop the fine motor ability necessary to make individual letters at different times. Somewhere between two and three years, children develop the ability to hold a pencil. But before a child is able to write independently, an adult can transcribe the stories that their young children are telling. An adult can write underneath a child's scribbles the ideas a child tells about his prewriting. When adults do this, the child is encouraged to continue using writing to convey his message. Just like reading, the more they find pleasure and encouragement in the writing process, the child will continue to engage in emergent writing behaviors.

When children begin to write their letters, they make frequent reversals in their letters (e.g., b for d and u for n) and often write their letters all over the page (as opposed to being fixed to a line). As children begin to sound out words, they will invent their own spellings and often only write the consonant sounds that they can hear. As children's writing ability improves, parents can gauge where a child is in the process of decoding.

Children continue to learn that written words symbolize spoken words. They also learn that everyone must combine symbols (letters) in the same fashion for the symbols to make sense. If they want others to understand their writing, they must use the same system of letters and words. When children are just beginning to write, it is not necessary to correct grammar or spelling. That will come later. For now, applaud your child's meaningful attempts at lasting communication.

As children begin to break the code of reading, somewhere between the ages of four and five, writing experiences can be introduced into a child's daily routine. Writing activities help children learn letter names and how to sound out new words. Writing also helps children understand that the written word is a way to express one's ideas. To facilitate emergent writing, consider the below points:

• Create an art and writing kit for the car. An inexpensive pencil box or ziplock bag filled with paper, pencils, and art supplies encourages children to not only write and create but also pass the time of a car ride.

- Young children can keep a journal. They can use pictures, scribbles, or even a word or two to document about each day. Caregivers can assist by writing a sentence or two underneath the scribbles making for a lasting keepsake of childhood.
- Help your child write their names on their artwork. The first word most children learn to identify is their own name. Your child's desire to write his name will increase as he/she understands that their name tells others about them!

When young children begin to demonstrate an interest in learning to write, they can do the following:

- They can practice in finger paint, shaving cream, pudding, applesauce, whipped cream, frosting, yogurt, water (on the sidewalk with a squirt gun), salt, flour, or sand.
- Children can practice their letter writing in the air using a pointer, an unsharpened pencil, their finger, their toes, or their elbow.
- Constructing letters using Q-tips, pipe cleaners, pretzel rods, blocks, chopsticks, toothpicks, play dough, string cheese, straws, uncooked spaghetti, twigs, yarn, dominoes, or rubber bands are exciting challenges for preschoolers.
- Children can decorate preprinted letter shapes by coloring or gluing items onto the letter. Try gluing items that start with the letter for added benefit (e.g., Apple jacks or apple seeds on the letter A). Figure 2.7 provides some suggestions to get your imagination going.
- Magnetic letters on your refrigerator or a cookie sheet allow your child to play with the letters. Help them sound out the combinations they place together. Try reading nonsense words too—the letters' sounds continue to stay the same. Other suggestions for making use of those magnets are found in figure 4.6 in the next chapter on play.
- Encourage your child to write letters, thank you notes, or e-mails to family, friends, or a pen pal. Children feel incredibly special and rewarded when they receive mail in return.

The most important outcomes of the early reading experiences of early childhood are the abilities to read and write. When children learn that they can share their words and ideas at a young age, they are destined to read, write, and preserve their ideas in print indefinitely. When children discover that their words have lasting value, they have found a way to say, "I matter."

Letter	Glue on:
Aa	acorns, apple seeds, apple jacks,
Bb	buttons, bubble wrap, band-aids, bird seed
Cc	cotton balls, candy corn, coffee grounds (dry)
Dd	dots (from bingo dabbers), dog food, dot candy
Ee	eyes (googly), easter grass, elbow macaroni
Ff	feathers, foil, felt, fingerprints, Fruit-Loops®
Gg	glitter, gems
Hh	hay, holly, Hershey Kisses®
Ii	insects (plastic), ink,
Jj	jewels, jelly beans
Kk	kite string, kidney beans (dried)
Ll	leaves, lace, lima beans (dried)
Mm	marshmallows, money (play), macaroni
Nn	noodles, nuts, nickels
Oo	oatmeal, oyster crackers
Pp	pasta, pom-poms, pennies, popsicle sticks, pebbles, pretzels, popcorn
Qq	q-tips, quarters
Rr	ribbon, rocks, ric-rac, rings, rice
Ss	star, stickers, seeds, sand, straws, salt, staples
Tt	tissues, toothpicks, tape
Uu	umbrellas (that you put in drinks)
Vv	valentines, velvet, velcro
Ww	wallpaper, worms (gummy)
Xx	x-rayed bones (milkbones painted white)
Yy	yarn
Zz	zippers, zoo animal stickers, zebra stripes

Figure 2.7. Help your child decorate an alphabet letter with these items of the same sound. For example, our letter "Y" has been covered with yarn.

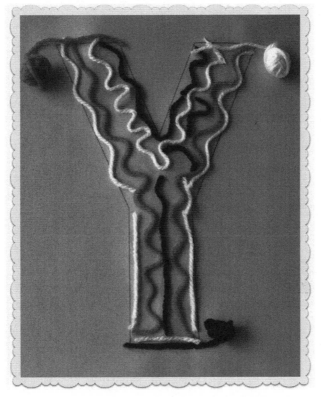

Photo 4. Help your child decorate an alphabet letter with an item of the same sound. Here, the letter "Y" has been covered with yarn.

NOTES

1. R. Anderson, E. Hiebert, J. Scott, and I. Wilkinson. *Becoming a Nation of Readers: The Report of the Commission on Reading, U.S. Department of Education* (Champaign-Urbana, IL: Center for the Study of Reading, 1985).

2. National Research Council, *Preventing Reading Difficulties in Young Children* (Washington DC: National Research Council, 1998).

3. L. Baker and A. Wigfield, "Dimensions of Children's Motivation for Reading and Their Relations to Reading Activity and Reading Achievement," *Reading Research Quarterly* (1997): 452–477.

4. Jim Trelease, *Why Read Aloud to Children*, Last modified 2014, http://trelease-on-reading.com.

5. C.E. Snow, M.S. Burns, and P. Griffin, *Preventing Reading Difficulties in Young Children* (Washington DC: National Academy Press, 1998).

Chapter Three

Just Play!

If we think back to our own childhoods, it is with nostalgia that we recall hours of unstructured time simply playing. We spent our summers outdoors initiating games and largely directing our own play. As parents, we have failed to duplicate the carefree play time of youth. The decline in children's play is well documented. Compared to children of the 1970s, children today spend 50 percent less time in unstructured outdoor activities.[1] Through our play, we were burning calories and staying healthy. The average ten- to sixteen-year-old today spends an average of thirteen minutes a day in physical activity and a whooping ten *hours* of their awake day motionless.[2] It is no wonder that physicians warn that today's children are destined to live shorter lives than their parents.

It is not just a child's physical health that suffers with the loss of play. While the result of childhood obesity is catastrophic, it is through play that children learn to socialize with others, solve problems, and invent. When children are at play, they are motivated from within to be successful. They work toward an end and pursue their own goals. Young children learn about their world through play and exploration. The American Academy of Pediatrics recommends that children spend at least sixty minutes of each day in open-ended unstructured play.[3]

Young children who spend time in free play use more sophisticated language, solve more problems, and use a higher-level thought process. The list below offers a complete list of attributes that child development specialists attribute to the power of play.

Long-term research has looked at play-based kindergarten versus kindergarten programs claiming to be "early learning centers" that started teaching

- Social Interaction
- Problem Solving
- Creativity
- Imaginative Role Play
- Language Development
- Self-Esteem
- Muscle Development
- Reasoning
- Responsibility
- Sharing
- Enjoyment
- Cooperation Mastery
- Experience
- Discovery
- Self-Expression

Figure 3.1.   Child development specialists list these gains for children who partake in a regular diet of free play.

phonics and other skills. By age ten, the children who had "played" excelled over their peers in a host of ways. They were more advanced in reading and mathematics. They were both socially and emotionally better adjusted in school. They excelled in creativity, intelligence, oral expression, and "industry."[4]

Play in early childhood is vital for many aspects of young children's physical, social, and emotional development. More specific developments are listed below:

- Language Development: As children pretend, they develop their verbal skills by taking on new roles, such as a cowboy, doctor, or astronaut. In their play they learn to use new vocabulary in appropriate ways. They may adapt the words used by a teacher or a princess.
- Cognitive Development: When children play without instruction, they develop their imaginations. They often use creativity and cognitive skills to make objects and people represent things. Pretend cowboys may turn a broom handle into a horse and an astronaut may use a box as a rocket ship. A budding doctor may use a stick as a thermometer. As children act out different scenarios, such as being in the classroom or having a tea party, they move the story along by imagining what might be said next. By acting,

children are gaining an understanding of how stories work. Pretend play allows children to learn the rules for different types of social situations. Children want to play because they have more control over their pretend worlds than they do over their real worlds and as such can take risks without fear of failure.

- Physical Development: Running, jumping, and climbing make children stronger and allow them to burn calories. Skipping or riding bikes helps them learn to balance. Throwing balls and building with blocks develop coordination.
- Social/Emotional Development: Through play, children work through situations that are difficult for them, perhaps the birth of a new sibling, loneliness, or the death of a beloved pet. Play has even been used by therapists as a healing tool for children who have been abused. As children age, they can learn to share and how to interact appropriately with others. They also learn the consequences of not interacting appropriately.

Children's play changes as they grow and develop. Children may participate in several of these play forms at any given time.

- Unoccupied play: In the early months of infancy, from birth to about three months, your child is busy in unoccupied play. Children seem to be making random movements with no clear purpose; this is the initial form of playing.
- Solitary play: From three to eighteen months, babies will spend much of their time playing on their own. During solitary play, children are very busy with play and they may not seem to notice other children sitting or playing nearby. They are exploring their world by watching, grabbing, and rattling objects. Babies and young toddlers have limited social, cognitive, and physical skills, making interactive play difficult.
- Onlooker play: Onlooker play happens most often during the toddler years. The toddler watches other children play. They are learning how to relate to others and also learning language. Although children may ask questions of other children, there is no effort to join another's play. While this type of play usually starts during the toddler years, it can take place at any age.
- Parallel play: From the age of eighteen months to two years, children begin to play alongside other children without any interaction. This is called parallel play. Parallel play provides your toddler with opportunities for role-playing such as dressing up and pretending. It also helps children gain the understanding of ownership. Children in this stage use the word "mine"

frequently. Children are beginning to show a preference for playing with other children of their own age. Parallel play is usually found with toddlers, although it happens in any age group.

Toys for young children need to match their stages of development and emerging abilities. Many safe and appropriate play materials are free items typically found at home. As you read the following lists of suggested toys for children of different ages, keep in mind that each child develops at an individual pace. Items on one list, as long as they are safe, can be good choices for children who are younger and older than the suggested age range. While the below listed toys are sure to be favorites, they are offered as examples only. Children outgrow their toys very quickly, so economy should be considered when purchasing. Not all toys need to be new. Resale shops, garage sales, and swapping with friends can save money. Simply use the tips given in figure 3.2 before giving the toys to your baby.

Before children are able to play on their own, responsive caregivers are the best playthings in early childhood. The amount and quality of the child–adult

There are two basic steps to cleaning baby toys:

1. Cleaning by scrubbing with soap and warm water. This removes any dirt and washes off germs. Using regular dish soap is all that is necessary.

2. Sanitizing goes a step further by killing dangerous germs. Before sanitizing, be sure to clean the toys. An inexpensive, effective and safe sanitizing solution can be made from diluting household liquid chlorine bleach—1 tablespoon of bleach in 1 quart of water or ¼ cup of bleach in a gallon of water. Properly diluted bleach is considered non-toxic and safe for cleaning children's toys. If you choose to use other approved sanitizing solutions, be certain the label states they are non-toxic and follow the directions carefully.

Depending on the size and material of the toy:
- Plastic toys that don't have batteries can be easily washed in the dishwasher with dish detergent and hot water. This cleans and sanitizes them.
- If you don't have a dishwasher, you can wash plastic toys in the sink with a clean sponge or rag, soap and warm water. After washing, sterilize the toys by dipping them in the diluted bleach solution, and let them air-dry in a dish rack.
- For toys with batteries or large plastic, metal or wooden toys, clean the outside with soap and water, then wipe with the bleach solution and let air-dry.
- Fabric toys may be washed in the laundry with laundry soap and hot water.

When to clean toys:
- When you notice they're soiled (after spit up or food is spilled)
- When your baby is recovering from an illness such as diarrhea or a cold.
- After a play date, when other children have put your baby's toys in their mouths.
- On a regular basis (every month for example)

Figure 3.2.   Babies are constantly touching things and putting their hands and objects in their mouths. Because they can pick up germs and illnesses easily, reduce your baby's chance of becoming infected by illnesses by keeping toys and equipment clean.

interaction, and not the cost of a child's toy collection, is paramount. The most educational thing parents can do for their children is to get down on the floor and play with them.

YOUR YOUNG INFANT—BIRTH THROUGH SIX MONTHS

Baby's eyes, ears, nose, hands, and mouth are their play tools. They use their bodies to make discoveries. As they grow, they will reach and grasp, allowing them the ability to explore the world in new ways. Your baby will learn about "cause and effect" and discover "object permanence" (that what he can't see does still exist). Their ability to communicate with you during play will grow from the use of gestures, facial expressions, sounds, and maybe even some words.

Babies are born with reflexes (actions that they do automatically) that can be a sort of play time. Early interactions with caregivers help a baby feel connected to their nurturers and world. Put your finger in your newborn's palm, instinctively she will grasp your finger.

Until they are three months old, babies have difficulty focusing on objects in the distance. Therefore, they prefer objects with strong color contrasts like black and white or white and red. Slowly move a colorful object in front of your baby's field of vision from about ten to twelve inches away. Move the object up and down or right to left. Your baby is learning to track objects using his eyes. Or, hold a rattle in each hand and shake one until your baby focuses on it. After a few seconds, shake the second rattle, allowing the baby to redirect their attention and focus.

When babies place toys in their mouths, they are exploring their world. There are a lot of nerve endings in that tiny mouth which tells their brain a lot about an object. Teething, which typically begins around four months of age, can be soothed by mouthing an object. Be sure you offer only safe objects for the baby's mouth and remember to clean toys regularly by following the directions given in figure 3.2 to keep your little one healthy.

Tummy time helps develop important muscles in the baby's neck and trunk. As he gets stronger, your baby will begin lifting himself up and eventually will reach for toys. Learning to move in new ways expands your baby's thinking skills. If he starts to fuss, pick him up or return him to his back.

When playing with your infant, do the following:

- Allow your baby to be a learner. Even though they cannot yet answer, ask them questions and comment on the activity you are both involved in. Call attention to one sense at a time.
- Choose play times when your little one is interested and involved.

- Repeat activities to firm up those neural pathways.
- Hold interesting toys just out of the baby's reach so they have to stretch and manipulate their fingers in order to grasp them. (If the baby becomes frustrated, move the item into the baby's grasp.)
- Encourage active exploration and investigation by keeping restraints like playpens and strollers to a minimum.
- Be sensitive to your baby's need for quiet time. The human brain needs time to organize itself and process learning. A baby who is cranky may just be overstimulated and need a break or nap.

What can I do with my young infant?

- Hold, rock, and sing to her.
- Take her outside on pleasant days.
- Explain what you are doing throughout the day when you change or feed her.
- Lay her on a big piece of paper and talk about the crunching noise when they move.
- Play different kinds of music on the radio and sing to her.
- Give her soft toys (like a stuffed animal or a clean sock) to hold and feel.
- Give her toys she can move and make noise with (like a rattle). Before giving any toy to a young child, assure it is not a choking hazard. Below is additional information regarding toy safety.

The Small Objects Tester was designed by the Consumer Product Safety Commission. It allows parents to test the safety of small toys, toy parts, or other small objects. If an object fits entirely inside the Choke Tester, then it's a choking hazard to a young child.
http://onsafety.cpsc.gov/wp-content/uploads/small-parts-tester300.jpg

The small part tester is a 2.25 inches long by 1.25 inches wide cylinder. This conforms to the approximate size of the average 3-year-old's throat. For comparison, the opening is slightly wider than a quarter or about the width of two fingers.

Many parents use a toilet paper roll as an inexpensive make-shift small parts tester. However, a toilet paper roll is wider and longer than the official tester.

If a toy or a piece of a toy intended for a child younger than 3 fits fully into the cylinder, that toy is banned by federal law. The law which has been around for decades has helped prevent children from choking on products. Small parts can get stuck in a child's throat and be deadly.

Age labels on toys are not based on a children's intelligence, instead they are for your child's safety. If a toy warns that it's not for children younger than 3, then really, that toy is NOT safe for young children.

Where siblings are present, the warning label should caution all in the household to keep track of the parts in the older child's toy. Be cautious to store those items out of a younger child's reach.

Figure 3.3. Small toys and small children can be a deadly combination.

The United States Consumer Product Safety Commission regulates products that are intended for use by children under three by federal law.These products include articles such as toys, dolls, puzzles, nursery equipment, infant furniture and equipment such as playpens, strollers, baby bouncers and exercisers. The regulation aims to prevent deaths and injuries to children under three from choking on, inhaling, or swallowing small objects they may "mouth". or that produce small parts when broken. The Commission defines a small part as:

- A whole toy or article
- A separate part of a toy, game, or other article
- A piece of a toy or article that breaks off during testing that simulates use or abuse by children

In an effort to guide parents and other consumers to the correct toys for different ages the CPSC advocates for proper labeling of toys. In addition to small parts, the CPSC also regulates other common requirements for children's products: lead, lead in paint, phthalates, and tracking labels.

Figure 3.4.   The United States Product Safety Commission assists consumers with regulations as well as a definition for a small object. If a toy, or a piece of a toy, can fit in the Small Object Tester, do not allow it in your baby's reach.

Photo 5.   Small object tester.

Photo 6.   Photo of a small toy warning label.

- Hang large pictures of people and animals at her eye level to look at.
- Coo and talk to your baby. Imitate her sounds and wait for her to imitate yours.
- Play peekaboo by hiding your face behind your hands or a onesie as you dress your baby. Initially your baby may simply pay close attention, but as she grows she may smile and squeal.
- Babies love when you lift their arms in the air and ask "How big is Baby?" Answer for your baby with "Soooooo Big!" Eventually, your baby will learn to lift their own arms in response to your question.
- Hold the baby in your arms in front of the mirror. Talk about and point to her body parts—eyes, nose, mouth, arms, and so on. Then step away from the mirror and ask, "Where did baby go?" Move back in front of the mirror and say, "There's the baby!"
- Sing songs like "Rain, Rain Go Away" and "Itsy Bitsy Spider" with your baby. Try using hand gesture while you sing—your baby loves to watch you entertain her.
- Carry your baby in a laundry basket on top of the warm clothes from the dryer. Be sure the clothes are not so high that your baby could fall out! Say the names of family members as you fold the clean clothes.
- Stroke her legs or feet with pleasant textures like a feather, velvet, cotton, and a soft brush. Talk about the different sensations.

Toys for Young Infants

As with all toys, the best are those that are open-ended and encourage a child to manipulate, interact, or learn something. Try to keep toys that claim to teach skills to babies at a minimum. Too often these toys have a "right" way to be played with. Toys with right answers do not allow for a little one to interact. Babies are sociable creatures. Typically, newborns most like the following:

(1) to look at things that are new and different,
(2) toys that are moving,
(3) toys that make noise,
(4) patterns of bright colors or black and white that resemble faces, and
(5) toys with different textures that they can feel.

Good toys for young infants include the following:

- toys they can reach for, hold, suck on, shake, and make noise with—rattles, large rings, squeeze toys, teething toys, soft dolls, textured balls, and vinyl and board books,
- books with nursery rhymes and poems, as well as recordings of lullabies and simple songs,
- pictures of faces hung so the baby can see them. Unbreakable mirrors also fascinate babies.

YOUR OLDER INFANT, SEVEN TO TWELVE MONTHS

Older babies appreciate the chance to discover how things work. They are solving problems through trial and error. The pincer grasp is the use of the pointer finger and thumb to pick up very small objects. This takes a lot of muscle coordination and eventually allows babies to begin picking up smaller objects. In the second half of their first year, little ones are developing this grasp.

Babies this age will roll, sit up, crawl, pull up, cruise along furniture, and sometimes begin to walk. Because these new physical skills are exciting for babies and offer new freedom, allow and encourage active play. Children need to be moving, exploring, and experimenting to learn how to problem-solve.

Older babies seem to be continually on the move. They quickly progress from rolling over to sitting and scooting. Quickly they are bouncing, creeping, pulling themselves up, and standing. They understand their own names and other common words. Some older infants can identify body parts, find hidden objects, and put things in and out of containers.

When playing with your older infant,

- Have a clean space in which your baby can crawl.
- Put bright toys near the baby so he can reach out or move toward them.
- Keep toys on open shelves as opposed to a tight-fitted toy box which discourages investigation.
- Put a big cardboard box on the floor to crawl inside and play.
- Put some chair cushions on the floor. Your baby can bounce and roll on them.
- Offer light blankets and scarves for your baby to hide under.
- Household objects like cooking utensils, bowls, and gadgets allow for creative problem-solving.

- Blow bubbles for your baby and try to catch a bubble so that it is sitting on the bubble wand. Encourage your child to reach out and pop the bubble or even catch some of their own. Activities like this also build hand-eye coordination.
- Seat your baby in his high chair. Meanwhile, squirt some dish detergent in a large plastic bowl, run water into the bowl, and make lots of bubbles. Scoop a handful of bubbles out and put them on baby's high chair tray. Watch him touch and explore, but be careful he doesn't eat them!
- Older infants love to use their hands and fingers for pushing buttons, opening boxes, and turning pages. Old calculators, keyboards, and phones (without batteries) are of interest to older infants.
- Sit on the floor and sing clapping songs together like 'Pat-a-cake, pat-a cake'. These will boost the baby's language skills and his hand-eye coordination.
- In each opening of a muffin tray, place an object that is yellow, for example. You could place a banana, a yellow teether, some yellow fruit loops, and a yellow mitten or sock. Let your baby touch and play with these objects, and repeat the word "yellow" as he explores the objects. Try making trays of different colored objects.
- As you restock your changing table or diaper bag, ask your baby to help you. Count the diapers out loud as you stack them together.

Toys for Older Infants

As with all toys, the best are those that are open-ended and encourage a child to manipulate, interact, or learn something. Try to keep toys that claim to teach skills to babies at a minimum. Too often these toys have a "right" way to be played with. Toys with right answers do not allow for a little one to interact. Babies are sociable creatures.

Typically, older infants most like the following:

(1) toys they can interact with,
(2) toys that are linked from cause to effect,
(3) toys that involve matching,
(4) toys that are moving and which they can push or pull, and
(5) toys that make noise.

Good toys for older infants include the following:

- toys that encourage pretend play like baby dolls, puppets, vehicles, and water toys,
- items that can be "put in," "taken out," and "sorted" into plastic bowls like large beads, balls, and nesting toys,

- building toys such as large soft blocks and wooden cubes, and
- toys that keep them moving like large balls, push and pull toys, and things to crawl over.

YOUR TODDLER, TWELVE TO THIRTY-SIX MONTHS

Typically, one- and two–year-olds can walk steadily and even climb stairs. They enjoy stories, say their first words, and can play next to other children (but not yet together). They like to experiment, but need adults to keep them safe. Because toddlers are better able to communicate and use their whole body, their play opportunities are unlimited. In addition to running, jumping, and climbing, one- and two–year-olds can use fingers and hands to play with smaller objects. Toddlers are beginning to understand the concept of "pretend." Their play is no longer based on imitation alone; young children of this age are using their whole body and imaginative mind to learn. Older toddlers in their second year are eager for playmates. They are beginning to play with other children. There is also growth in their ability to use their imaginations. Two-year-olds often spend a lot of time in pretend play, playing "house" or "mommy" to their own baby doll.

When playing with your toddler, do the following:

- Action games like "Ring Around the Rosie" and "London Bridge" encourage children to move, sing, listen, take turns, and cooperate.
- Pretend your child's teddy bear is real and make her walk, go to bed, and do other everyday activities. Talking about what you are doing so your toddler will understand that you are "pretending" will help her begin to develop her own imagination.
- Toddlers love to play simple games of hide and seek. Take turns hiding under the bed sheets in the morning or, at bath time, use a big towel to hide under.
- Sit across from your child with your feet touching. Roll a ball to each other. This activity is great for building arm muscles and hand-eye coordination. For variation, roll a large car or play truck to each other.
- Assuming your toddler is walking (although some may not be), go for a walk together, and take a bucket or basket along. Aid your child as they collect small objects that are of interest like stones, leaves, or pine cones. While your child may enjoy carrying the bucket or basket, don't be surprised if she dumps its contents and starts collecting them all over again.
- Play music that encourages particular actions like stamping as an elephant or tiptoeing like a mouse. Marching to music or following the directions of a song are great fun for a toddler.
- Balloons are great for indoor play because they move slowly enough to be chased and are relatively easy to catch. Count how long it takes for the

balloon to float down to the ground or how long it takes your kiddo to catch it. Balloons require close supervision. Be careful that the balloon does not go into your child's mouth, as a broken balloon is a choking hazard. Pick up any broken balloons from the ground as well. Animals, birds, and fish can also choke on swallowed balloon pieces.

- Newly mobile, toddlers love to be chased and to be caught, especially when he gets a big bear hug and slobbery kiss. For variation, pretend to be different types of animals like a roaring lion or a flying eagle. Sometimes, let your child chase you too. This is great exercise for everyone!
- Cut a hole in the middle of the lid of a clean ice cream container. Together, look around the house for items your child can put through the hole. Clothespins and hair curlers are two suggestions. Assure these items do not fit through a choke tube.
- Fill big buckets or tubs with water. Use measuring spoons and cups, plastic bottles, and sponges to play with the water. Be careful your excited toddler does not slip as the floor gets wet.
- Together, paint with shaving cream tinted with food coloring. For easy cleanup, play during bath time and "write" on the bathtub walls.
- Make a texture book for your child. Cut shapes from a variety of textured fabrics and papers such as lace, satin, cotton, corduroy, sandpaper, corrugated cardboard, and so on. Glue these into a book and write the texture on each page ("silky," "scratchy," etc.).
- Staple together six pages of construction paper (red, orange, yellow, green, blue, and purple) to make a book. Write the appropriate color's name on each page. Let your child color pictures on each page. For example, on the red page draw an apple, on the orange a pumpkin, yellow would have a sun and moon, green may offer a tree, on blue draw a fish, and on the purple page include grapes. Read your book together. As an alternative, take six photos of your child wearing a shirt of each color and glue those to the appropriately labeled pages.
- Turn a big cardboard box into a barn. With your child, walk and "talk" like an animal, perhaps meow like a cat or "trot" and neigh like horse.
- Color one side of a paper plate red and write the word "stop" on it. Color the other side green and write the word "go." If you'd like, glue a Popsicle stick to the bottom so you can easily hold it. Let your child pretend to be a car (encourage him to make *vroom, vroom* or *honk, honk* noises). You will be the traffic light. Your child has to stop at the red sign and can go at the green sign. Once your child has the hang of this game, see if he'd like to tell you when to stop and go. When your child can master this walking, try playing as your child rides a toy.
- Take old shoeboxes and cut a hand-sized hole in the side of each. Put a different interesting item inside each box (e.g., a few acorns, some crinkly

leaves, or a stick). Have your child put his hand inside and touch the object without looking. Can he guess what is inside?

- While out in a stroller or waiting at an appointment, play "I Spy." Tell your baby you spy an object of a certain color. Challenge them to look around the room and guess what it is you see. As your child becomes comfortable with the game and has the verbal skills, allow them to do the spying. As an alternative, use a flashlight to play the game at night. The child can shine the light on what he thinks you are spying.
- Encourage pretend play by providing dress-up clothes and other props. When you assume a role, you can expand on your child's ideas and keep the dialogue going.
- Into the second year, fine motor ability may allow your older toddler to draw pictures and play with sand or play dough. Providing art supplies like paper, crayons, play dough, and paints will let young imaginations soar. Provide your child with her own supplies for writing or drawing. From a shoebox or other container, create an art and writing kit for your child. Allow your child to decorate her kit and label it with her name.
- Older toddlers may be interested in a playdate. Invite a friend over to play or visit the neighborhood park or library, giving your child a chance to play in new ways. Stay close by to help your child learn to share and to resolve conflicts; children this age have a difficult time understanding that other children have feelings too.
- Cut doors and windows in a cardboard appliance box. Together with your toddler, draw on it with crayons or "paint" it with water and big brushes or sponges. Turn into a car wash for all the vehicles your toddler can now drive in for a wash.
- Put pillows, cushions, or a mattress on the floor and jump away!
- Have your toddler choose a color and celebrate it all day long. For example, if he chooses red, wear red and have strawberry jam on your PB&J sandwich. Later, finger paint a red painting, pick some red flowers, and count red cars on the way to the grocery store.
- Join your toddler in a scribbling game. Mark your paper with different colors and shapes. Don't worry about drawing a picture; instead, just have fun developing your child's hand movements.
- Cut pictures of animals out of magazines or buy a pack of animal stickers. Glue them to sturdy cardboard. Make sure there are matches like two pictures of horses, two pictures of sheep, and so on. Lay these pictures out (face up) on the floor and see if your child can match the animals that are the same. As your child gets older, turn the cards upside down to pay a memory match game. Or, challenge your child to find all the animals that start with a particular letter or would live on a farm, a zoo, and so on.

Interesting and challenging play materials in a children's home after the first year predict the child's later IQ and future school achievement in both reading and math.[5] Open-ended toys, as opposed to those with screens, buttons, or plugs, are still best. When purchasing toys for your toddler, choose toys that are versatile and are able to be used in different ways. Typically toddlers love to take things apart and put them back together. They love opening and closing, putting in and taking out. Choose toys that can be used in different ways from one day to the next. For example, plastic nesting cups can be used as pretend dishes, to build a tower or for water play.

Consider looking for toys that will age along with your child. Look for toys that can change their purpose at different development levels. For example, stuffed animals can be used to play house, to create a zoo, or as puppets to retell a story.

Toddlers are rapidly learning language. They eagerly test the limits physically: jumping from heights, climbing, and rough-and-tumble play. Their sense of danger is limited, so adults need to keep a close eye on their explorations. They have good control of their hands and fingers and like to do things with small objects.

Good toys for toddlers include the following:

- items for creating like wide, nontoxic, washable markers or crayons, finger paint, play dough, large paint brushes, colored construction paper, toddler-sized scissors with blunt tips, a chalkboard and large chalk, and rhythm instruments;
- toys for pretending such as toy phones, dolls, baby carriages and strollers, dress-up clothes, puppets or stuffed toys, plastic animals, and vehicles;
- construction supplies such as cardboard and wood blocks; These can now be smaller than the ones used as a baby.
- toys that use their large and small muscles like puzzles, large pegboards, toys with parts that do things (dials, switches, knobs, lids), large and small balls for kicking and throwing, ride-on equipment (but probably not tricycles until children are three), tunnels, and pounding and hammering toys;
- toys that require active handling like nesting toys, stacking toys, and toys for stringing and sorting; All such toys teach about relationships and offer opportunity to talk about concepts like big, bigger, full, empty, and so on. According to the National Association for the Education of Young Children, these concepts as well as those given in figure 3.5 are perfect math concepts to include in our everyday play with toddlers.
- toys that require solving problems like wood puzzles, blocks that snap together, and things with hooks, buttons, buckles, and snaps;
- pretend and building toys such as blocks, smaller transportation toys, construction sets, child-sized furniture (kitchen sets, chairs, play food), dress-up clothes, and sand and water play toys;

Math talk enriches play for toddlers. Weave the following math concepts into your play with young children:

- Number and operations—understanding the concept of number, quantity, order, ways of representing numbers, one-to-one correspondence (that one object corresponds to one number), and counting.

  "You have two eyes, and so does your bear. Let's count:--1, 2."

  "I have more blocks than you do. See, I have 1, 2, 3, and you have 1, 2. I'm going to put one back in the box. Now I have the same as you!"

- Shapes and spatial relationships —recognizing and naming shapes as well as recognizing the relationship between objects and space.

  "The wheel rolled under the couch and the rest of the wagon is on top!"

  "The red ring is next to the blue ring."

  "Some of the beads we have today are square, and some are round."

- Measurement—size, weight, quantity, volume, and time.

  "Moving that tractor is hard. It is heavy."

  "You played with your Lincoln-Logs for a long time today!"

  "Let's count how many animals make up that long line."

- Patterns, relationships, and change—recognizing and creating repetitions of objects, events, colors, lines, textures, and sounds; understanding that things change over time.

  "Dolly has stripes on her shirt—white, blue, white, blue, white, blue."

  "Let's tap the spoon to the beat of this song."

  "I put the blocks in the bucket; you dump them out. I put the blocks back in the bucket; you dump them out!"

- Collecting and organizing information—gathering, sorting, classifying, and analyzing information to help make sense of what is happening in the environment.

  "The big lid fits the big bowl and the small lid fits the small bowl."

  "The dolls are on the first shelf.The balls need to be put in a basket before they can go on the shelf."

Figure 3.5. The National Association for the Education of the Young offers five math concepts that can be woven into our everyday conversations and play with toddlers.

- Your "real" stuff, which your toddler also wants to play with(like your cell phone, television remote, garage door opener, and keys); When household items need to be replaced, consider removing batteries and placing in your child's toy collection.
- "Ready to Read" toys like magnetic alphabet letters and alphabet blocks are now appropriate. Real take-out menus, catalogs, junk mail, or magazines are fun for your child to look at and use in their play. Suggestions for putting magnetic letters to use throughout early childhood are given in figure 3.6.
- Sensory play includes any activity that stimulates your young child's senses: touch, smell, taste, sight, and hearing. Caregivers can stimulate and excite the senses by creating sensory-tub or sensory-table activities. Children naturally use the scientific processes while they play, create, investigate, and explore. Adults can make sensory tubs or add items like those below to purchased sensory tables to facilitate their child's natural curiosity. See figure 3.7 and also photos 7 and 8.

Magnetic letters can be played with on any metal surface but cookie sheets fit well in children's laps.

- Find Me A - For early letter-learners, ask "Can you find me a letter 'O' or 'M'?" Offer a choice between two letters to allow for success.
- Spell Your Name - Use letters to spell your child's name, then; mix the letters up. Help your child move the letters back to spell their name.
- Find Look-Alikes - Using duplicate letters, encourage your child to find the matches.
- Beginning to Spell - Spell out colors, animals, or things that your child will recognize.
- Alphabet Order - When your child knows the names of each letter and the Alphabet Song, help your child put the magnetic letters in alphabetical order.
- Take Turns Letter Search - Pick out the letter A and ask your child to find the next letter (B). Keep adding letters until you finish the alphabet.
- Letter Sort - Ask your child to organize the letters in groups based on the letters features. For example, some letters have straight lines, others are curved, some are open shapes, and some are closed shapes.Some letters even look they same when you turn them upside down.
- Fish for Letters - Put the letters in a pile and have your child pick out a letter as you call out the letter's name.
- Is It Capital or is it Lowercase? - Ask your child to sort the letters into groups of uppercase letters and lowercase letters.
- Write Words - Spell some words with your magnetic letters and ask your child to copy the words onto a piece of paper (Or in finger paint, sand, etc.)
- Color Words - Spell the colors (red, blue, white, etc…) as you draw a picture of something that is the chosen color.
- Spell the Numbers - Write a list of numbers for you child on paper (use the numeral and the word) and help your child copy the word with the magnets.
- Word Families - Show your child how you can change an entire word by changing or (adding letters.) For example "MAD" becomes "BAD" when you change the M to a B; or, "MAD" can become "MAID" when an "I" is added between A and D.
- Rhyme Time - Use letters to spell a three-letter word (cat, dog, pig, fan, etc). Ask your child to think of words that rhymes. If desired, spell the rhyming word below the initial word.
- Uppercase and Lowercase Match - Have your child match the uppercase letters with the lowercase
- What's Missing - Arrange the alphabet letters in order. Have your child close their eyes and remove one (or more) letters. Ask your child which letters are missing.
- Real or Made-Up - Create several 'real' words that are easy to read, and add in a few non-sense words that follow the same word family pattern. For example:cat, bat, rat, zat, wat. Ask your reader which words are real and which are nonsense.
- One or More - Practice adding an 's' to words. With just one letter, they can read–and create–a whole new word!
- Ready to Spell - For an older kiddo who has mastered simple Spelling Lists, ask her to spell that week's list on the fridge.
- Beginning and Endings - Add a prefix like 're' on the tray then add 'do' to make 'redo'. Then leave 're' on and add 'view'. Play with different prefixes (pre-, un-, mis-) and suffixes (-y, -less, -ful).

Figure 3.6. Twenty different ways to play with magnetic letters.

What is a sensory bin or table? It is usually a large plastic container that you fill with some kind of textured medium. Commercially sold tables are available to purchase as well. Throw in a couple of play toys and you have a sensory bin.

Sensory bins are great for kiddos because they receive tactile stimulation and it encourages imaginative play. While you may cringe at the thought of a bin of dry rice or cooked spaghetti on your living room carpet, plastic table clothes from a dollar store or old shower curtain protect your floors. Or, move your bin outside when weather permits.

Some things to keep in mind when creating your own sensory play opportunities:

- Choking hazards, if your child is still putting everything into their mouth, be mindful of what you are putting into the bin or hold off on this play until it is safe and enjoyable.
- Some textures have a shelf life, you may need to recycle or replenish them.
- Never force a child's hand into a texture. If they don't like it or are having a hard time touching, be respectful. Don't give up, maybe your child needs to use a shovel instead of their fingers. Over time a child may step out of their comfort zone. This bravery is a lesson of it's own that makes the mess of some bins worthwhile.
- Have towels ready for wet textures. (Letting a nervous child know that a towel is available may help them feel more comfortable touching the texture.)

There is no "right way" to design or present sensory play. Your plastic tub, wading pool or store bought sensory table will provide your child with hours of learning, exploring and fun.

When a child loses interest (perhaps after a week or so), change mediums and materials to excite their curiosity and coincide with a child's interests. Here are some ideas to get started:

Examples of Mediums:

- water (with or with soap)
- snow
- ice
- sand (wet or dry)
- cornmeal
- rice or pasta (cooked, uncooked, and/or dyed)
- hay
- beans
- shaving cream
- whipped cream
- confetti, glitter or sparkles
- potato flakes, sugar or salt
- packing peanuts
- cotton balls
- beads
- (water beads)
- craft pom-poms
- rocks, stones or gravel
- Easter grass or colored confetti

Figure 3.7. The ideas for sensory play are endless and are only limited by a caregiver's imagination (and budget).

To Dye Uncooked Rice or Pasta

Need: 1/4 cup rubbing alcohol, 1T food coloring, 2 cups rice (or pasta), 1 qt Freezer bag
Pour alcohol and food coloring into the bag and mix together. Add uncooked rice (or pasta). Zip bag closed. Let set until rice (or pasta) has reached the desired color. Pour onto wax paper lined trays to dry.

To Dye Sand

In a large ziplock bag mix sand and paint together. Zip up the bag. Shake, kneed, and mix the sand and the paint. Only add a little bit of paint at a time till you have the desired color.

After choosing your medium, add items for the child to sift, dig, and manipulate. Small plastic shovels, rakes, tweezers, magnifying glasses, strainers, measuring cups, spoons, squeeze bottles, tongs, funnels and ladles are all terrific for exploration.

The possibilities for filling your sensory bin are endless and can change according to a child's interests. As with any play experience, after a child has lost interest, make a change to reignite curiosity.

Below are some ideas for getting started:

THEME	ITEMS TO ADD
Apple Pie	uncooked oatmeal, cinnamon sticks, plastic apples, measuring spoons and cups, pie tin, trees, tractor, plastic worms
Autumn	plastic leaves, pine cones, sticks
Bees	black beans, yellow porcupine balls, plastic bees, sunflowers, honey pot, honey stick, wagon wheel pasta noodles
Birthday	confetti, birthday candles, gift bows, balloons, birthday party hat, cupcake holders
Christmas	tinsel, bells, beads, glitter snowflakes, an array of ornaments boxes, small pine boughs
Dinosaurs	sand, plastic dinosaurs, fossils, rocks, paint brush, little eggs, mimi trees
Easter	Easter grass, chicks, rubber ducks, bunnies, plastic Easter eggs, strawberry baskets
Farm	popcorn, farm animals, fences, tractors, feathers, raffia, silo
Gardening	potting soil, birdseed, small shovels, watering cans, fake flowers on stems, small plastic bugs like caterpillars, planting pots
Halloween	black beans, plastic pumpkins, orange pompoms, skeleton bones, green pipe cleaners
Ocean	water, shells, fish, mermaids, fish bowl plants, bowls, nets

Figure 3.7. (continued)

THEME	ITEMS TO ADD
Pirates	black beans, dress-up necklaces, marbles, pirate figurines, velvet bag of gems, treasure box, coins, rings, "X"
Pond	aqua colored water beads, lily pads from foam shapes, plastic plants and flowers, fish, duck, turtle, dragonfly
Space	black turtle beans, planets (super balls), Glow In The Dark or foil stick stars, rockets, astronauts, marbles, jacks, balled up tin foil, rocks
Winter	flour, (or, real snow if available) arctic animals, snow plows, sifters, foam snow flakes

As children get older, your sensory bin can develop along with them. For your older child, support learning concepts with multiple senses. Multiple senses will be each creating stronger and stronger brain connections in your child. Below are some ideas to get your imagination flowing.

THEME	ITEMS TO ADD
Alphabet Letter	Using alphabet blocks for your medium, hide items that start with one letter sound; "M" for example: mirror, monkey, mail, money, mouse, milk caps "P" for example: pumpkin, peppermint, present, pig, pan, pail
Are You My Mother (book)	bird seed, cow, hen, cat, birds, dog, boat, airplane, nest, egg, baby bird
Chicka Chicka Boom Boom (book)	Alphabet beads, brown pipe cleaners, acorns (coconuts), shells, flowers from leis
Cloudy With a Chance of Meatballs (book)	cooked spaghetti, , brown pompoms, wooden spoon,plastic food, cars, trees,
Human Body	kidney beans, googly eyes, pink yarn (intestines), red and blue pipe cleaners (veins), teeth, plastic bones, surgical tools, heart
Red (choose a color)	red pompoms, red popsicle sticks, red buttons, apples, hearts, cherry and watermelon erasers
Robots	sparkly pompoms, silver pipe cleaners, toy gears and wheels, googly eyes, nuts, screws, screwdriver, buttons, old remote controls (with batteries removed), bottle caps
The Very Hungry Caterpillar (book)	green rice, large bottle tops, lolly pop sticks, colored pompoms, plastic fruit, cakes, ice creams and other food items from the story, caterpillar, butterfly
The Wizard of Oz (book or movie)	yellow legos, silk poppies, lion, tiger, bear, emeralds, farm house, little basket, black dog, oil can, little diploma, heart, broom, wand
Weather	blue aquarium rocks, cotton balls, blue beads (rain), silver pipe cleaners (lightening), sun, snowflake shapes, plastic cubes (ice), rainbow colored pompoms

Figure 3.7.

Photo 7.　A pirate-themed sensory bin for preschool.

*Photo 8.　A sensory bin based on the story **Are You My Mother?**.*

YOUR PRESCHOOLER, THREE TO FIVE YEARS

When playing with your preschooler, do the following:

- Preschool children like to jump, ride tricycles, and play ball. Toys that encourage large muscle activities integrate two-sided body coordination as well as exercise. These activities are making important brain connections between both sides of the brain.
- Preschoolers who like to play with water or sand are ready for utensils that are more difficult to manipulate like eggbeaters, watering cans, squeeze bottles, and funnel.

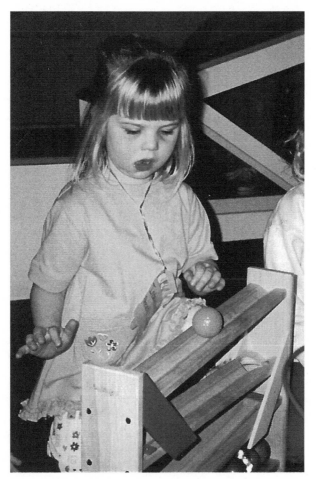

Photo 9.   Experimenting with ramps and gravity.

- Now that your child can blow their own bubbles, spills will be plentiful so you may wish to make your own soap bubbles. Add 3/4 cup of liquid dish soap to two quarts of water. Help your child blow bubbles with small plastic containers that are open at both ends like frozen juice containers. They can also use straws or green plastic berry baskets. (Because they love bubbles, let your child wash some of your unbreakable dishes.)
- Let your child play with sand in buckets. Give her scoops, muffin tins, funnels, rolling pins, and salt shakers to use.
- Preschoolers like to pretend. Encourage your child to take on other's roles so they learn empathy. "Let's pretend I am the baby and you are the Mommy (or Daddy) today." Pretending helps a preschooler's imagination grow.
- Preschoolers are learning (although they have not perfected) how to share.
- Children like choices in their play. "Would like to play with the play dough or finger paint?" Or "Would you rather use the red or yellow paint?"
- Preschoolers like to make more complicated things with blocks and Lego. Check to make sure that any wood they use is smooth and free of splinters.
- Board games and card games like "War" and "Go Fish" will entertain your preschooler while preparing them for future math lessons. First grade math achievement can be predicted by how many board and card games a child has played before school entry.[6] Family game night is not only a time for bonding but a time for playful learning.
- Children are now beginning to manufacture their own pretend play by imitating their own experiences. For example, after visiting an ice cream parlor, a child may be seen playing an ice cream shopper. To allow their imagination to flourish, assist them by providing a table, clean ice cream containers, an ice cream scoop, and cones made from paper. Children playing make-believe in this way are engaging in dramatic play.

DRAMATIC PLAY

Dramatic play is play that is deliberately designed so that children can imitate other people they have observed in their everyday experiences. It is a purposeful attempt to link language experiences to play exploration. Young children, usually beginning around age three, enjoy pretending to be others. Dramatic play provides unlimited interaction with oral language.

Referring back to the necessary literacy skills for reading readiness, it is easy to see how dramatic play provides an avenue for meeting each concept. For demonstrative purposes, imagine a young child is playing in a pretend kitchen that has been set up by a caregiver to mimic a pizza restaurant.

Photo 10.   Playing "Row, Row, Row Your Boat."

(1) Narrative Skill: The child answers a pretend-telephone, takes an order, creates the pizza, and sends the pizza off for delivery. Through this fantasy, children learn that stories need a "beginning," "middle," and "end." Children learn that things must happen in a logical sequence.

(2) Print Motivation: In the kitchen a child may offer a customer a scribbled menu and take down that customer's order on a pad of paper. They may refer to a written recipe and create a bill to go out with the delivery boy. The child has experienced meaningful uses of the written word in their play.

(3) Vocabulary: Children will use words necessary in their play environment. These words may not be words a child is likely to use in day-to-day conversation. Expressions like "For Delivery" or "Pick-Up Only" could be used in our example. Words unfamiliar to the child, like provolone, mozzarella, pepperoni, spicy, well-done, and so on can be used by the adults that are engaged with the child of this play scenario.

(4) Print Awareness: Our pizza parlor might be equipped with wall signs like "Place Your Order Here," menus, pizza boxes, employee name tags, discount coupons, and a pencil and a notepad for taking orders. While the child playing in the center may not be able to read all the words, they are aware that the words belong in this environment and convey meaning to all who enter it.

(5) Letter Knowledge: Perhaps "Papa's Pizza Parlor" specializes in pepperoni pizza. The /p/ sound can be explored and identified in the sur-
roundings. "May I please take your order?" Incorporates another /p/ into
our pizza shop play.

(6) Phonological Awareness: Children may want to develop names for the
different pizza products they sell. Using rhyming adjectives, they are
manipulating sounds and developing an awareness of syllables: "Tasty
Pizza," "Pasty Pizza," "Flakey Pizza". Or, a jingle for their pizza com-
mercial can be clapped out in rhythm: "Get your pizza, while it's hot.
Dough in the oven, sauce in the pot. Yum-yum-yummy. I like it a lot."

Planning play like in the example above can revolve around many
themes and are limited only by the adult's imagination. Adults should be
cautioned that pretend play is not gender specific. Boys enjoy playing in
a kitchen as much as a girl may enjoy playing in a garage. Preschool is an
opportunity for all children to try on many different roles. Both boys and
girls should be encouraged to interact with science items like telescopes,
microscopes, and science kits. Prop boxes enable children to act out what
they know, practice words in a meaningful context, and play different
roles. Be sure to include literacy items in prop boxes and play areas. If
possible, storing toys by theme in old computer paper boxes will make
set-up time for the adult much smoother. Label the boxes and rotate them
into play to prevent boredom. Be cautious not to stereotype. Both sexes
can enjoy playing in a flower shop or gas station. Early play in no way
indicates later sexual preferences. Like the pizza shop example above,
other themes that can be pulled together in dramatic play prop boxes are
listed in figure 3.8.

After children have explored different play themes, reading children's
books set in those places further extends language development. Essential
literacy skills will be reinforced as the child talks to their caregiver about the
similarities of their play experiences and the ones they see in their books.
Visit your local library to find titles that fit your needs. Children's librarians
are knowledgeable and a great help in locating picture books for young children about almost any subject. The titles given in figure 3.9 are perfect for
expanding preschool play.

Another variation of dramatic play is to use a story book as your play
inspiration. For example, after reading "The Three Little Pigs," act out the
story using stuffed animals, plastic toy animals, or sock puppets. Later, during
block play, build houses and pretend to "Huff and puff and blow the house
down." Before nap, ask your child to tell you the story about the pigs and
wolf. If possible, have flannel pieces and a flannel board for your child to use.
Or, allow them to draw the illustrations and use them to tell you the story.

Other classic stories that lend themselves to dramatic play are suggested in figure 3.10.

Dramatic play obviously builds imagination and develops social skills, but it also promotes physical development as children button, tie, and snap clothing and costumes. It also reinforces math skills when children count money,

Theme	Items to include:
Airplane	tickets, passports, backpacks, chairs, seat numbers, snacks and beverages, microphone, stuffed animals
Bank	play money, deposit and withdraw slips, check book, calculator or adding machine, rubber stamps and ink, coin rolls, paper and pens
Beach	towels, blanket, picnic basket, buckets and sand toys, sunglasses, empty sun tan lotion bottles, beach ball, shells, shell identification list, beach rules, lifeguard whistle, postcards, travel magazines, camera
Camping	tent, flashlight, binoculars, nature books, sleeping bag, thermos, fly swatter, small cooler, pretend food, maps
Car Wash	tricycles,buckets,water,buckets,sponges,squeegees,hose,car wash signs,play money, receipts, air fresheners
Construction Site	hard hat, ruler, tool belt, tools, blocks for building, blueprints, clean paint brushes, empty paint cans, paint samples, tape measure
Fire Station	raincoat, boots, old vacuum hose, phone, fire hat, flashlight, walkie-talkies, fire safety posters, map
Flower Shop	plastic flowers, cash register, money, phone, order book, plastic vases, seed packets, watering can, ribbon
Gas Station	tools, tool box, play money, cash register, bucket and squeegee, car keys, rags, auto supply catalog, funnel, tire pump, poster with prices
Grocery Store	play food, cash register, paper bags, play money, sale flyers, coupons, grocery cart, purses or wallets
Hair Salon	plastic combs and brushes, mirrors, rollers, spray bottles (empty), appointment book, magazines, empty shampoo bottles, towels, telephone, plastic capes, ribbons,
Hospital	lab coats (or white shirts), surgical gloves, surgical masks, scale, meal tray, measuring tape, gauze, cotton balls, splints, crutches, doctor's kit (include stethoscope, bandages, band-aids, medicine bottles, tongue depressors, plastic test tubes, roll of masking tape to be cut and used as band-aids), dolls, medical bracelets, slings, thermometer, white sheets, blankets, blank booklet (for patient chart), clipboards, file folders, magazines, prescription pad
Ice Cream Parlor	ice cream scoops,paper cones, empty ice cream tubs, play money/cash register, apron and hat, order pads/pencils, wipe-off board menu, empty whipped cream spray cans, bowls ,toppings, sprinkles

Figure 3.8. Some examples of items to include in your prop boxes for dramatic play.

Library	books, recorded stories, stuffed animals, alphabet posters, felt board and pieces, puppets, reading glasses, stamps for marking books, cards for books, magazines, bookmarks, pencils, pens, stickers, ABC index cards, file folders, posters of children's books, telephone, library cards, book bags, name tags, computer
News Show - Weatherman	maps, pointer, suit jacket or dressy shirt, video camera (optional),weekly forecast chart, weather symbols for the map (sun, clouds, snowflake, raindrops, etc.), weather pictures for "on-location" reports
Pet Store	stuffed animals, small bowls for food and water dishes, ribbon, yarn, or rope for collars and leashes, boxes, plastic tubs, baskets for cages, books about pets, play money, signs—store name, animal labels, pet care instructions, bags of food—paper lunch bags stuffed with newspaper, price tags, receipts
Police Station	pads for writing tickets, pens, clipboard, police hat and badge, 911 signs, walkie talkies, license plates
Post Office	paper, envelopes, saved junk mail, cardboard or small boxes, stickers to use as stamps, a shoe box to act as a mailbox, bag or basket for delivering the mail
Restaurant	play food, menus, signs, aprons, table chef's hat, kitchen towel, small notepad for taking orders, pretend money, play tablecloths and dishes, coupons, signs
School	chalkboard/chalk, notebooks, pencils/paper, books, backpack, lunchbox, chairs, teachers desk, flag, papers, red pen, grade book, computer
Travel Agency	globe and/or maps, brochures of vacation places, old telephone, calendar, travel magazines, atlas, books about places, posters, plane tickets, passports, schedules/itineraries, postcards
Veterinarian's Office	stuffed animals, gauze, cotton balls, pamphlets about animals, empty medicine bottles, pet brushes, stethoscope, prescription pad, appointment calendar

Figure 3.8. (continued)

set menu prices, and make change in the pretend store. It promotes reading and writing as children develop their own props including signs for a car wash, menus for a restaurant, and books for their house.

Good toys for preschoolers include the following:

- toys for solving problems like puzzles (now with up to twelve to twenty pieces), blocks that snap together, collections to sort by length, width, height, shape, color, smell, quantity, and other features. For example, collections of plastic bottle caps, plastic bowls and lids, keys, counting bears, or small colored blocks.
- toys for pretending and building more complex structures. Smaller Lego blocks, transportation toys, construction sets, child-sized furniture,

Theme	Titles to include:
Bank	Brisson, Pat. *Benny's Pennies*. New York : Doubleday Books for Young Readers, 1993. Carlson, Nancy. *Start Saving, Henry!* New York : Viking, 2009. Sirimarco, Elizabeth. *At the Bank*. Chanhassen, MN : Child's World, 2000. Wells, Rosemary. *Bunny Money*. New York : Dial Books for Young Readers, 1997.
Beach	Cash, Megan Montague. *I Saw the Sea and the Sea Saw Me*. New York : Viking, 2001. Heiligman, Deborah. *Fun Dog, Sun Dog*. New York : Marshall Cavendish, 2005. Hubbell, Patricia. *Sea, Sand, Me!* New York : HarperCollins Publishers, 2001. Schertle, Alice. *All You Need for a Beach*. Orlando, FL : Silver Whistle/Harcourt, 2004.
Camping	Berry, Lynne. *Duck Tents*. New York : Henry Holt and Company, 2009. Cousins, Lucy. *Maisy Goes Camping*. Cambridge, MA : Candlewick Press, 2004. Coyle, Carmela LaVigna. *Do Princesses Make Happy Campers?* New York: Taylor Trade Publishing, an imprint of The Rowman & Littlefield Publishers Group, Inc, 2015. Lakin, Patricia. *Camping Day*. New York : Dial Books for Young Readers, 2009. Singer, Marilyn. *I'm Gonna Climb a Mountain in My Patent Leather Shoes*. New York: Abrams Books For Young Readers, 2014.
Construction Site	Barton, Byron. *Machines at Work*. New York : Crowell, 1987. Hearn, Sam. *Busy Builders*. New York: Cartwheel Books, an Imprint of Scholastic, 2016. Meltzer, Lynn. *The Construction Crew*. New York : Henry Holt & Company LLC, 2011. Ready, Jean. *Busy Builders, Busy Week!* New York: Bloomsbury Children's Books, 2016. Steers, Billy. *Tractor Mac: Teamwork*. New York: Farrar Straus Giroux, 2016. Savage, Stephen. *The Mixed-Up Truck*. Brookfield, CT: Roaring Brook Press, 2016.

Figure 3.9. Suggestions to extend dramatic play through children's literature.

Fire Station	Beaty, Andrea. *Firefighter Ted.* New York : Margaret K. McElderry Books, 2009.
	Finn, Rebecca, *Busy Fire Station.* New York: Sterling Children's Books, 2016.
	Goebel, Jenny. *The Firefighter.* New York: Grosset & Dunlap, an imprint of Penguin Group (USA) LLC, 2015.
	Hubbell, Patricia. *Firefighters: Speeding! Spraying Saving!* Tarrytown, NY: Marshall Cavendish Children, 2007.
	Rockwell, Anne. *At the Firehouse.* New York : HarperCollins, 2003.
Flower Shop	Bruce, Lisa. *Grow Flower, Grow!* (Originally titled: *Fran's Flower*) New York : Scholastic, 2001.
	Cimarusti, Marie Torres. *Peek-a-Bloom.* New York : Dutton Children's Books, 2010.
	Ehlert, Lois. *Planting a Rainbow.* San Diego, CA : Harcourt Brace Jovanovich, 1988.
	Wellington, Monica. *Zinnia's Flower Garden.* New York : Dutton Children's Books, 2005.
Gas Station	Borass, Tracey. *Auto Mechanics.* Mankato, MN : Bridgestone Books, 1999.
	Ditchfield, Christin. *Oil.* New York : Children's Press. 2002.
	Gibbons, Gail. *Fill It Up! All About Service Stations.* New York : T.Y. Crow-ell, 1985.
	Shulman, Mark. *Gorilla Garage.* New York : Marshall Cavendish, 2009.
Grocery Store	Dewdney, Anna. *Llama, Llama Mad At Mama.* New York : Viking, 2007.
	Firestone, Mary. *Supermarket Managers.* Mankato, MN : Bridgestone Books, 2003.
	Greene, Carol. *At the Grocery Store.* Chanhassen, MN : Child's World, 1999.
	Maccarone, Grace. *I Shop With My Daddy.* New York : Scholastic, 1998.
Hair Salon	Ehrlich, Fred. *Does a Yak Get a Haircut?* Brooklyn, NY : Blue Apple Books, 2003.
	Moss, Miriam. *Bad Hare Day.* New York : Bloomsbury Books : Distributed to the trade by Holtzbink Publishers, 2003.
	Rim, Sujean, *Birdie's Big-Girl Hair.* Boston, MA: Little, Brown, 2014.
	Savadier, Elivia. *No Haircut Today.* New Milford, CT : Roaring Book Press, 2005.
	Sirimarco, Elizabeth. *At the Barber.* Eden Prairie, MN : Child's World, 2000.

Figure 3.9.   (continued)

Pizza Shop	Asch, Frank. *Pizza*. New York: Aladdin, 2015.
	Oxley, Jennifer. *Peg & Cat: the Pizza Problem*. Cambridge, MA: Candlewick Entertainment, 2016.
	Steig, William. *Pete's a Pizza*. New York : HarperCollins Publishing, 1998.
	Walter, Virginia. *"Hi" Pizza Man*. New York : Orchard Books, 1995.
	Wellington, Monica. *Pizza at Sally's*. New York : Dutton Children's Books, 2006.
Police Station	Hubbell, Patricia. *Police: Hurrying! Helping! Saving!* Tarrytown, NY : Marshall Cavendish Children, 2008.
	Meadows, Michelle. *Traffic Pups*. New York : Simon & Schuster Books for Young Readers, 2011.
	Simon, Charnan. *Police Officers*. Chanhassen, MN : Child's World, 2003.
	Staniford, Linda. *Police to the Rescue Around the World*. New York: Heinemann Raintree, 2016.
Post Office	Bee, William. *Stanley the Mailman*. New York; Peachtree Publishers, 2016.
	Carter, Don. *Send It!* Brookfield, CN : Roaring Book Press, 2003.
	Minden, Cecilia. *Letter Carriers*. Chanhassen, MN : Child's World, 2006.
	Poydar, Nancy. *Mailbox Magic*. New York : Holiday House, 2000.
	Taback, Simms. *I Miss You Every Day*. New York : Viking, 2007.
Veterinarian's Office	Huneck, Stephen. *Sally Goes to the Vet*. New York : Harry N. Abrams, 2004.
	Landau, Orna. *Leopardpox*. New York: Clarion Books, Houghton Mifflin Harcourt, 2014.
	Lee, Chinlun. *Good Dog, Paw*. Cambridge, MA : Candlewick Press, 2004.
	Leonard, Marcia. *The Pet Vet*. Brookfield, CT : Millbrook Press, 1999.
	Minden, Cecilia. *Veterinarians*. Chanhassen, MN : Child's World, 2014.

Figure 3.9.

dress-up clothes, dolls with accessories, puppets and puppet theaters, and sand and water play toys are all enjoyed by preschoolers.
• toys to create with like large and small crayons and markers, large and small paint brushes and finger paint, big and small paper for drawing and painting, colored construction paper, preschooler-safe scissors, chalkboard with chalk, modeling clay and play dough, modeling tools, paste, scraps for collages, and a workbench with a vise, hammer, nails, and saw.

In addition to these suggestions, children can retell any story using felt pieces, drawings, puppets, stuffed animals or (especially as they get older) just words.

- Brett, Jan. *Goldilocks and the Three Bears*. New York : Penguin Group, 1992.

Make bowls of oatmeal and vary the temperatures – hot, cold and "just right". Practice testing chairs in your home to find the one that is most comfortable. At nap or bed time, find the bed that is most comfortable. Bring a stuffed animal to bed that you can pretend to scare right out the door.

- Eastman, Philip D. *Are You My Mother?* New York: Random House Books For Young Readers, 1960.

Match up toy animals with potential mommies. Look in magazines and identify moms with their children. Have the animals ask each other, "Are you my mother?"

- Galdone, Paul. *The Gingerbread Boy*. New York : Houghton Mifflin Harcourt, 2006.

Use cookie cutters to make a play-dough gingerbread boy and several animals. Allow the cutouts to chase each other. Have your gingerbread boy race against the other characters. Have your child chase you saying "Run, run as fast as I can, you can't catch me I'm the gingerbread mom (or dad)." Reverse and chase your child.

- Galdone, Paul. *The Three Billy Goats Gruff*. Houghton Mifflin Harcourt, 1981.

Make a bridge out of couch cushions and pretend to cross it. Throughout the day ask "Trip, trap who's that walking down my steps?" or "Trip, trap who's that coming into my kitchen?"

- Galdone, Paul. *Three Little Kittens*. New York : Houghton Mifflin Harcourt, 1988.

Hide three pairs of mittens around the house for your child to find. Eat a messy food item wearing an old pair of mittens and talk about what happens. Hang the mittens outside to dry after rinsing them out. Eat pie!

- Marshall, James. *Red Riding Hood*. New York : Penguin Group, 1987.

Pack a picnic basket and share lunch. Pretend to be the wolf and steal the basket. Hide under the bed covers, pretending to be the wolf. As you play hide and seek, say "Oh Baby, what big eyes you have. What big ears you have." And so on.

- Rathmann, Peggy. *Good Night, Gorilla*. New York : Puffin Books, 2000.

Be the zookeeper and line up all the stuffed animals that will follow you home from the zoo. Pretend to put your stuffed animals to asleep and say goodnight to each animal that has followed you to bed.

- Slobodkina, Esphyr. *Caps For Sale: A Tale of a Peddler, Some Monkeys and Their Monkey Business*. New York: HarperTrophy, 1938.

Play monkey see, monkey do. Imitate what your child does and then reverse. Practice balancing hats or pillows on your head as you walk. Pretend to sell the hats off your head, "Pillows, pillows for sale. A penny for a pillow."

- Stevens, Janet. *The Princess and the Pea*. New York : Holiday House, 1989.

Stack up pillows or blankets and lay on them. Place an object like a large bead or block under different cushions and see who can feel it. Sleep on top of the bead during nap time.

Figure 3.10.   Dramatic play with classic children's tales.

- musical toys like rhythm instruments and keyboards, xylophones, maracas, and tambourines.
- toys for using both large and small muscles such as balls for kicking and throwing and catching, ride-on equipment including tricycles, tunnels to crawl through, climbers with soft material underneath, wagons and wheelbarrows, plastic bats and balls, plastic bowling pins, and targets and things to throw at them.

THOUGHTS CONCERNING ORGANIZED SPORTS FOR YOUNG CHILDREN

Registering preschoolers or kindergarteners into team sports is wonderful for social interaction, learning rules, and cooperation. The basic skills of running, catching, throwing, kicking, and moving bilaterally are all important for future athletic ability and the skills that will eventually evolve into becoming an athlete. However, preschool is not the time to focus on winning. Instead, organized sports pose the opportunity to learn that you do not always win but games are still fun. Team sports should not take the place of free and pretend play.

Children in this age group who play together can often be seen making up their own "rules" for games. Following the rules is important to preschoolers. While the rules may not make sense to adults, as long as the children agree to follow the rules, all is well.

TECHNOLOGY, DVDS, "APPS," AND GAMING SYSTEMS, OH MY!

In 2009, The Walt Disney Company began offering refunds for all the "Baby Einstein" videos that did not make babies into geniuses. They may have been a great electronic babysitter, but the refunds appear to be an admission that they did not affect intellect. The videos, essentially simple productions featuring music, puppets, bright colors, and not many words, became a staple of baby life: A study in 2003 reported that a third of all American babies from six months to two years old had at least one "Baby Einstein" video.

In fact, studies link significant television viewing to decreased language skills. The American Academy of Pediatrics recommends no screen time at all for children under age two. Despite that recommendation, of children aged two or younger, 59 percent watch TV daily and 42 percent watch a

DVD daily. The average zero to two year old spends approximately two hours and forty-five minutes a day watching television or DVDs. The greatest educational damage comes from what is *not being done* during those hours of sitting in front of the TV: conversations not held, games not played, drawings not drawn, and books not read. Keeping young children's electronics to a minimum is wise. Real intelligence comes from real experiences with real people.

Whether the television is on for a few or many hours in your home, one thing should be done to make the most of it whenever it's in use: turn on the closed captioning. Small doses of captioned television will do no harm and will help with reading just by exposing children to print. Captioning is available for free via the menu button on the TV remote. It is also available on most DVDs.

Far more than any electronic device, playing with a nurturing and attentive caregiver enhances language development, social competence, creativity, imagination, and thinking skills. [7] Technology fails to add the main ingredient necessary for language and early literacy: namely, the back and forth that is required in human interaction. Even with the programming abilities of the best programmers, multimedia for children only offers a scripted experience. Children cannot deviate from the designers' intended conversation. A child's interests and experiences cannot be expanded. So while multimedia may be just fine for all children of a given age range, it will never be just right for your child.

All parents universally want that which is best for their children. We often want them to grow faster, read earlier, and solve math problems sooner. Toy manufacturers know this and often market high-priced toys that play by themselves with no child needed! There is no need to spend a fortune on toys to give your child the best possible play experiences. You are the best toy for your child! Long after toys and technology are stored in a closet, the experiences your child has shared with you will be remembered and evident in their eventual school success. Play on!

NOTES

1. T.F. Juster, F. Stafford, and H. Ono, "Major Changes Have Taken Place in How Children and Teens Spend Their Time," *Child Development Supplement* (2004).

2. R.S. Strauss, D. Rodzilsky, G. Burack, and M. Colin, "Psychosocial Correlates of Physical Activity in Healthy Children," *Archive of Pediatric and Adolescent Medicine* (2001): 155, 897–902.

3. American Academy of Pediatrics, "The Importance of Play in Promoting Healthy Child Development and Maintaining Strong Parent–Child Bonds," *Pediatrics* (January 2007): 182–191.

4. L. Darling-Hammand and J. Snyder. *Handbook of Research on Curriculum* (New York: MacMillan, 1992).

5. J.M. Healy, *Your Child's Growing Mind: Brain Development and Learning From Birth to Adolescence* (New York: Broadway Books, 2004).

6. J.M. Healy, *Your Child's Growing Mind.*

7. D.P. Fromberg and D.F. Gullo. "Perspectives on children," *Encyclopedia of Early Childhood Education* (New York: Garland, 1992).

Chapter Four

A Literate-Looking Environment

Everywhere we go, we are surrounded by print. Print fills our homes and our communities. Every day we see labels on our food, logos of our favorite restaurants, traffic signs, and street signs. As adults we look at billboards, containers, posters, and computer screens, not registering that what we are really seeing are words. Instantaneously our brains are "decoding." Briefly, decoding is the process by which we turn each shape (marking) we see into a letter and each letter into a sound. We combine those individual sounds into a word and then assign an object, a feeling, or a concept to that word. Language only works when a group agrees to what those decoded words represent. A natural place for children to begin their understanding of the written word is in the words they see around them every day, their "environmental print." Young children find environmental print easy to read because it makes sense. When they read environmental print, it is tied to their everyday needs, experiences, and interests.

Reading research experts have classified print into two kinds: functional and environmental. Functional print is the print children need to read because it provides information they need to function. Examples of functional print are schedules, routines, labels, calendars, sign-in sheets, and so on. On the contrary, environmental print is the print in the background. They may not be in need of the information it provides, but without any effort, it is in their line of vision. Environmental print is the first print that children learn to "read."

As children develop, they internalize the decoding process, that symbols and letters have meaning. Initially, they may only be recognizing the colors and shapes of the logos they encounter often. But, being able to identify these symbols makes them feel successful and capable as readers. The more success they feel, the more they will strive to read. And the more they "read," the more connections they will create. They are connecting that the "K" in K-Mart

Heo, Yumi. *Red Light, Green Light.* New York: Cartwheel Books, 2015.

Hoban, Tana. *I Read Symbols.* New York: Greenwillow Books, 1983.

Searcy, John. *Signs in our World.* London: DK Children, 2006.

van Lieshout, Maria. *Backseat A-B-see.* San Francisco, CA: Chronicle Books, 2012.

Figure 4.1.   A sampling of children's picture books that explore signs in the environment.

has a /k/ sound. They recognize that the K in KFC stands for Kentucky, and Kentucky has the same /k/ sound. They have learned that K always makes the /k/ sound. Only twenty-five more letter-sound combinations left to learn. While we may be disappointed that the first words our children can read are McDonald's®, Coke®, or Wal-Mart, these familiar logos are terrific ways to encourage our young children to think about letters and letter sounds.

Children's books devoted to environmental print are available for children who show a special interest in signage and logos. Some suggestions are given in figure 4.1.

Environmental print is readily available to all children and their grown-ups. Not only is this reading material plentiful, it is completely free. The print in our environment provides us with unlimited opportunities to facilitate our children's interactions with letters, sounds, and words. Children who grow up in print- and literacy-rich environments *and* have conversations with their caregivers about the print around them are most likely to demonstrate emergent reading behaviors.[1] Use the suggestions below to make the most of the print in your environment.

READ EVERYWHERE YOU GO

You can find opportunities to read in the car, in the store, and at restaurants. These opportunities can become word games to play while on the go:

- Play a game during a long car ride where everyone reads the license plates of passing vehicles: "Everyone find an A, now a B," and so on.
- Choose a simple sign to focus on during one car trip (e.g., a stop sign). Have your child count the number of stop signs she sees during a ride. Have her read the sign. Point out that the sign says the same thing each time it is passed. Talk about the sound of the letters. "In stop, the S makes the /sssssssss/ sound. Sssssssss-top spells stop."
- Choose a letter of the day or week. Encourage your child to look around for things that start with that letter anywhere you go. Eat food that starts with

that letter. Write the letter in the air on the sidewalk with a spray bottle or sidewalk chalk. Point out that letter in the signs you pass. Use words that start with that letter in an exaggerated fashion. For example, "I /ffff/inally /ffff/igured out that we will have /ffff/ish sticks and /ffff/rench /ffff/ries for dinner tonight. It will be /ffff/antastic."

- Play "I Spy" with letters. At the grocery store or in the mall, let your child search for certain stores and products. Commend their "reading" when they are successful.
- After ordering in a restaurant, play "I Spy" with the signage around you. Instead of searching for items of a particular color, look for the letter "Aa." As children progress, you can look for lower or uppercase letters. Another variation is to "I spy something that starts with the /Aa/ sound."
- Have an alphabet "scavenger hunt." Look for letters hidden in objects like Os in tires, Ys in the forks of trees, Hs on a ladder, or Us in the playground swings.
- Engage in T-shirt reading. As people pass you in a store or park, read all the shirts that advertise a product or service or have sayings on them. Look through your family's clothing and read the words with your child. When you dress your child in readable clothing, be sure they know what it says.

Photo 11.   While waiting for his rice, this little one is using his chopsticks to make letters. Now they are an "X."

Photo 12. While this toddler is engaged at the aquarium, he can be asked to touch the Os on the tank. "Do you see the O shapes? They make the sound of wonder, 'Oh'!"

TAKE FIELD TRIPS

Take young children to places that will expose them to new words. Point out the signs. Often, the signs show pictures that relate. For example, at the zoo, the word monkey will have a monkey symbol next to it. The brain will associate the picture-and-letter combination.

Additionally, new locations will offer an opportunity to use new and unusual words (photo 13). For example, the words you use at an aquarium will vary greatly from those you would use at a farmer's market. On the way home, stop at your local library and pick up a picture book or two that reinforces the words you have just experienced. Some examples are listed in figure 4.2.

BE A READING ROLE MODEL

- More than anything, young children seek acceptance and praise. Your child wants to imitate you and be like you. Have plenty of reading material for yourself as well as for your child. Let your child see that you are reading often and enjoying books and other print. He will follow your good example and will be more likely to pick up a book for enjoyment, too. Establish a regular time and place for daily read-aloud sessions, such as before bed or during bath time.

Photo 13. This little one giggles at the feel of a goat during a visit to the petting zoo. Mom and son talk about the feel of the rough fur, the sharp horns, and perhaps the wet tongue.

Destination	Potential Environmental Print	Vocabulary Words to Use	Children's Book Titles	Follow Up Ideas
Airport	ticket, arrival, departure, luggage, claim, delay, flight, gate, runway	passport, counter, baggage, destination, round trip, tourist, travel, pilot	Brown, Lisa. *The Airport Book*. New York: Roaring Book Press, 2016. Downs, Mike. *The Noisy Airplane Ride*. Berkeley, CA : Tricycle Press, 2005. Hubbell, Patricia. *My First Airplane Ride*. New York : Marshall Cavendish Children, 2008. London, Jonathan. *A Plane Goes Ka-Zoom*. New York : Henry Holt, 2010.	Make paper airplanes, Hold out arms and pretend to "take off" and fly into the sky

Figure 4.2. A list of field trip destinations, with potential new vocabulary, along with ways to continue your conversations about your experience after arriving home.

Apple Orchard	acre, cider, Fuji, McIntosh, Granny Smith, Red Delicious	grove, cultivate, variety, pollinate, prune, core, crunchy, sort	Chernesky, Sanzari. *From Apple Trees to Cider, Please!* New York: Albert Whitman & Company, 2015. Hill, Eric. *Spot's Harvest.* New York : G.P.Putnam's Sons, 2010. *Pat the Bunny at the Apple Orchard.* New York: Golden Books, an imprint of Random House Children's Books, 2015. Wallace, Nancy Elizabeth. *Apples,Apples, Apples.* Delray Beach, FL : Winslow Press, 2000.	Make applesauce or apple pie, cut an apple in half using it as a rubber stamp with ink or paint
Animal Shelter	adoption, humane, donate, volunteers	shelter, community, needs, control	Graham, Bob. *Let's Get a Pup, said Kate.* Cambridge, MA : Candlewick Press, 2001. Jackson, Emma. *A Home for Dixie: The True Story of a Rescued Puppy.* New York : Collins, 2008. Jones, Val. *Who Wants Broccoli?* New York: Harper Collins Children's Books, 2015. Lombardi, Kristine A. *The Grump y Pets.* New York: Abrams Books for Young Readers, 2016.	Donate some change that child has earned to your local shelter, help a neighbor walk their dog
Aquarium	freshwater, saltwater, marine, ecosystem	ocean, lake, environment, sea, tank	Aliki. *My Visit to the Aquarium.* New York : HarperCollinsPublishers, 1993. Berenstain, Jan. *The Berenstain Bears at the Aquarium.* New York : Harper, 2012. Buzzeo, Toni. *One Cool Friend.* New York : Dial Books For Young Readers, 2012.	Purchase a fish bowl and goldfish for observation, put Swedish fish in blue jell-o
Bird Sanctuary	endangered, extinct, nestlings, species, native	garden, protected, adapt, chicks, nest	Harrison, George H. *Backyard Bird Watching For Kids* . Minocqua, WI : Willow Creek Press, 1997. Montenegro, Laura Nyman. *A Poet's Bird Garden.* New York : Farrar Straus Girouz, 2007. Tafuri, Nancy. *Will You Be My Friend? A Bunny and Bird Story.* New York : Scholastic Press, 2000.	Use feathers to paint, make and hang a bird feeder
Botanical Garden/Butterfl y House	rainforest, habitat, conservatory, life cycle, pupa, cocoon, flora, metamorphosis	Exotic, humidity, nectar, tropical, scales, antennae	Bunting, Eve. *The Butterfly House.* New York : Scholastic Press, 1999. Lerner, Carol. *Butterflies in the Garden.* New York : Harper Collins, 2002. Rosenberry, Vera. *Who Is In the Garden?* New York : Holiday House, 2001.	Find a caterpillar, watch it grow and transform into a butterfly, Make butterflies out of clothespins and coffee filters

Figure 4.2.

Children's Theater	entrance, performers, refreshments, orchestra	stage, intermission, drama, curtain	Bourgeois, Paulette. *Franklin's School Play*. Toronto : Kids Can Press, 1996. Cousins, Lucy. *Maisy's Show*. Somerville, MA : Candlewick Press, 2010. Holabird, Katharine. *Angelina on Stage*. Middleton, WI : Pleasant Company Publications, 2001.	Act out a favorite story, Pantomime different feelings like happy, sad or angry
Fish Hatchery	Trout, Salmon, watershed, natural resources, spawning	Stream, migrate, industry,	Cousins, Lucy. *Hooray for Fish!* Cambridge, MA : Candlewick Press, 2005. Ehlert. Lois. *Fish Eyes: A Book You Can Count On*. San Diego, CA : Harcourt Brace Jovanovich, 1990. Einhorn, Kama. *My First Book about Fish*. New York : Random House, 2006.	Play the card game "Go Fish", eat "Goldfish" crackers
Planetarium	astronomy, solar system, dome, constellations, observatory, telescope	stars, planets, sunrise, sunset, space	Carle, Eric. *Draw Me a Star*. New York : Philomel Books, 1992. Rockwell, Anne. *Our Stars*. San Diego, CA : Silver Whistle, 1999. Trapani, Iza. *Twinkle, Twinkle Little Star*. Boston, MA : Whispering Coyote Press, 1994.	Use a Lite-Brite toy to make constellations, use paper towel tubes to create a pretend telescope
Retirement Home	residents, assisted, medical, ambulance, station	elderly, seniors, retired,	Agee, Jon. *The Retired Kid*. New York : Hyperion Books for Children, 2008. Lakritz, Deborah *Say Hello, Lily*. Minneapolis, MN : Kar-Ben Pub, 2010. Orloff, Karen Kaufman. *I Wanna Go Home*. New York: G. P. Putnam's Sons, an imprint of Penguin Group (USA), 2014. Zolotow, Charlotte. *I Know a Lady*. New York : Greenwillow, 1984.	Visit an elderly relative, make cards holiday crafts to distribute at a local elderly community
Train Station	Conductor, Tunnel, Arrival, Departure, Passengers	trip, rails, caboose, engine, locomotive, transportation	Hillenbrand, Will. *Down By the Station*. San Diego, CA : Harcourt Brace, 1999. Sturges, *I Love Trains!* New York : HarperCollinsPublishers, 2001. Suen, Anastasia. *Window Music*. New York : Viking, 1998.	Line up cardboard boxes and make them into a train, practice blowing a whistle and hailing "all aboard"

Figure 4.2.

- Visit the public library, your local bookstore, and other places where books and reading are the focus. Get library cards for everyone in the family and use them often! Find out about programs available at the library and the bookstores and attend with your child. Children who see that books are everywhere and that there are books for every reader will value books and reading themselves.

- Share your favorite reading experiences with your child. Tell your children, "This was my favorite book when I was your age" or "I can't wait to start my new book."
- When you see your child absorbed in a book, stop what you are doing and ask questions or talk about the story. "What are you looking at, Tommy? Did you see the picture of the bulldozer on the page before this one?" Prompt your child's reading by asking them about what they see happening in the pictures. Children may also be encouraged to read to their pets or toys, such as dolls or stuffed animals.
- Set a family reading time where everyone sits together in the family room, the kitchen, or the backyard and reads! Take turns talking about what you are reading. Share paragraphs, sentences, descriptions, and words. Further, reinforce language and literacy skills by having family puzzle and game nights. Games like Memory®, Candy Land®, Old Maid®, Concentration®,

Photo 14.   This kiddo is sharing a holiday story with his best buddy who is also ready to listen!

Scrabble®, or Pictionary® are wonderful. If the youngest children cannot participate, they will still observe the importance of words as others play in their presence.

• Bring a book wherever you go and let your child catch you reading, as you wait in the carpool line at a sibling's preschool, as you wait for a doctor's appointment, or as she plays in your yard.

• Model reading and writing for pleasure and for specific uses, such as making a shopping list, reading the nutritional information on a food container, leaving notes for family members, making to-do lists, leafing through the mail, or writing a letter. As you are engaged in these activities, tell your child exactly what it is and why you are doing the activity. Point out how you are reading instructions, labels, and maps as well as all the other times you are using print to complete your daily tasks.

• As you make your grocery list, allow your child to make a picture grocery list with scribbles, letters, drawings, or cutting pictures out of advertisements. Or, place a large sheet of paper on the refrigerator. Each time an item is emptied and needs to be replaced, your child can glue or staple the label onto the paper. The paper can then be taken to the store. Your child can match the picture list with labels in the store and be a successful shopper worthy of your thanks for being such a wonderful helper. As you put away groceries, read each label. Encourage your child to "read" each label as he helps you put items away too!

• Unplug the TV! The television (and other such screens) is very too often the alternative to recreational reading. If TV isn't a choice, then reading just might be! Set the example by turning off the TV and choosing a book instead.

• Make books with your child. You can assemble scrapbooks or family photo albums together, look through them, and read the captions often. Write

Photo 15.   The title page of a preschooler's board book about his family is a timeless memento of playing together.

a book with your child about what you did today, or record a story and illustrate it. Use your digital camera to record a special trip or hike. Add captions to the photo prints and make a photo book. Easy directions for making your own board books are given in figure 4.3.

1. Decide on the size of your book, as well as the number of pages it will have. Add an extra 1/2 to 1 inch to the width for the binding. Add two additional pages to your total page count for the front and back covers.

2. Cut your pages out of thick cardboard (at least 1/16 inch), including the covers, into a square or rectangle using sharp scissors or a utility knife. You may want to round the top and bottom right-hand corners for a more professional look.

3. Stack the pages on top of each other, all facing the same direction, and trim so that all the edges line up as exactly as possible.

4. Decorate your pages as desired, gluing on photos, adhering stickers, drawing pictures or writing a story. Be sure to use non-toxic materials whenever possible, as board books often end up in a baby's mouth. Note that the left 1/2 to 1 inch of the page will be used to bind the book, so do not put any pictures or text in this area.

5. Cover the pages with laminating paper if desired.

6. Punch holes through one page, approximately 1/2 inch from the left edge of the page. Punch a hole every inch or so.

7. Trace the holes you punched in the first page onto your other pages to ensure that the holes line up exactly. Punch holes into all of your other pages, including the covers.

8. Stack all of the pages together in the order you want the book to be read, carefully aligning the edges of the book and the holes you punched.

9. Push a piece of yarn or string through the top hole from front to back. Make sure that the string is tight, but that the pages can still open to lay flat. Tie the ends in a tight knot against the spine of the book. Trim the edges. Repeat with the bottom hole, then alternate from top to bottom to keep the pages properly

10. Open your book so that it lays flat.

11. Cut a piece of fabric to fit from the open edge of the front cover to the open edge of the back cover, leaving about an inch on all four sides free for gluing.

12. Lay the fabric right side down in a horizontal rectangle. Open your book on top of the fabric with the spine of the book laid vertically near the middle of the fabric. Turn all the pages of the book to the left, exposing the inside of the back cover.

13. Apply glue to the edges of the inside back cover, covering about an inch of each edge with glue, and fold the right short edge of the fabric over onto the inside edge of the book.

14. Lift the book carefully and apply glue to the back cover, except for the spine. Lay the book down and press against the cover to glue the fabric to the cover, pulling the fabric taut to remove wrinkles.

15. Turn all of the pages to the right, exposing the inside of the front cover. Apply glue to the edge of the front cover farthest from the spine of the book. Again, cover about an inch of each edge with glue. Do not fold the fabric over yet.

16. Close the cover nearly all the way, keeping the edge of the book with the glue just barely open.

17. Apply glue all over the front of the cover.

18. Pull the fabric tight around the book and press the fabric onto the glue on the outside and inside of the front cover, pulling the fabric taut to remove any wrinkles. It is okay if extra fabric extends past the glued part. Trim excess fabric after the glue has dried.

Figure 4.3.   Follow these step-by-step instructions to make your own board books.

19. Open the book again and lay it flat. Pull the excess edges of fabric on the top and bottom over the inside edges of the front and back covers and glue them in place, snipping a small cut at the corners to help them lay flat.

20. Cut squares of decorative paper to glue over the fabric edges on the inside front and back covers if desired. Glue the squares of paper into place.

Allow all parts of the book to dry completely before allowing baby to handle it.

An alternative to making your own board book, is to buy blank board books from an online store such as Blank Slate Board Books at http://www.blankslatebooks.com/.

Figure 4.3.

CONSTRUCT A PRINT-RICH HOME

A print-rich environment is one in which children are purposely surrounded by many forms of text such as signs, labels, books, magazines, and other printed material. Print-rich environments help children connect that print is a mode of communication. Creating a print-rich environment is a caregiver's way of demonstrating to children that print communicates just as much as spoken words. When we construct a print-rich environment, we are deliberately encouraging children to interact with written language.

Label Your Child's Environment

- Choose an area in your home where your child spends the majority of his time. Ideally this would be your child's bedroom or play area.
- Create labels that can be hung on objects. In a bedroom, for example, "door," "closet," "dresser," "toy chest," and "lamp" could be identified with labels. When creating labels, print in a font that children can easily identify. Quality preschool classrooms are likely to employ this same technique.
- Tape the labels at your child's eye level and cover the labels in a laminating film or with scotch tape to improve durability.
- Add additional forms of print to the room. Place posters (ABC posters regarding your child's favorite interest are readily available), calendars, bulletin boards, books, magazines, toy catalogs, and other print material that your child finds interesting into the space. Don't be afraid to include logos of your child's favorite stores, restaurants, toys, or clothing.
- Take time to point out the labels to your child naturally. When they are looking for their blocks, you may say something like, "This word tells me that your toys are inside. The sign reads 'toy box.' I bet if we look inside we will find the box with b-l-o-c-k-s blocks in it. That is where we should search for your blocks." As you speak, point to the labels to which you are referring. Do not, however, make reading the labels a lesson.

- Be careful not to "overdo" things. Too much can be overwhelming.
- Change the print in your environment periodically. Labels, posters, and books left out for too long become "wallpaper" and stop being noticed. However, adding new words into the environment renews interest and starts conversations again!
- Write your child's name on his belongings and explain that D-a-w-n spells Dawn, and when others see D-a-w-n on a dolly accidentally dropped at the store, they will know to whom the dolly belongs.
- Place magnetic letters on your refrigerator or on other magnetic surfaces and use the magnetics as discussed previously in figure 3.6.
- Stencil your child's name on their door or hang wooden letters bought from the craft store.
- Use chalkboard or dry-erase paint on a door or wall and use it to write notes to family members. Read the notes out loud and allow your child to be a part of the note writing and reading.
- Have reading materials throughout your home. For example, scatter magazines on a coffee table, keep take-out menus in a stack near your phone, or include a basket of books near the toilet.
- When you are cooking, show your child the recipe and read it out loud as you prepare dinner, lunch, or make a birthday cake. Keep cookbooks out in the kitchen.
- Allow your child access (supervised if they are young) to a variety of writing tools like crayons, markers, pencils, and paper. Age guidelines are suggested in the chapter on play.
- Hang art with words. If your child is willing, she can tell you about her own artwork and you can write her description on the piece and hang it.
- Hang special occasion banners that announce "Happy Birthday" or "Happy New Year."
- Invest in letter-shaped cookie cutters and serve words made out of Jell-O or sugar cookie dough. (These make great additions to a child's play dough collection as well!)

Teachers relay that children who enter school with the literacy skills listed in figure 4.4 will be better prepared when it is time to begin formal reading instruction in the primary grades.

Children learn in the context of important relationships. Early care and nurture have a long-lasting impact on how infants develop, their ability to learn, and their capacity to regulate their own emotions. Nurturing a young child's early literacy skills is done through reading and talking to them every day, getting down on the floor to play with them, and fostering a home environment rich in print. Yet, doing these things does not teach them how to read. Instead, these developmentally appropriate activities are exposing our young

☐ Speaks in complete sentences
☐ Understands and follows directions with at least two steps
☐ Understands vocabulary related to position, direction, size and comparison (alike/different, top/bottom, first/last, up/down)
☐ Makes simple predictions and comments about a story being read
☐ Classifies (same/different, alike/not alike) objects by physical features:
☐ Recognizes, copies or repeats patterning sequence
☐ Demonstrates the ability to correctly put in order or sequence up to three story pictures
☐ Organizes objects that go together in groups
☐ Participates in repeating a familiar song, poem, finger play and/or nursery rhyme
☐ Retells a simple story after listening to a story
☐ Does simple puzzles (up to four 4 pieces)
☐ Identifies or points to five (5) colors
☐ Recognizes own name in print
☐ Points to and/or recognizes letters in own name
☐ Prints letters in own name
☐ Recognizes familiar signs, words and logos in the child's environment
☐ Identifies two words that rhyme/sound the same when given rhyming picture words
☐ Recognizes ten alphabet letter names (may include those in own name) by pointing to requested letter
☐ Matches ten letters with the sounds they makeUses symbols or drawings to express ideas
☐ Uses writing and drawing tools and child-sized scissors with control and intention
☐ Copies figures (line, circle, X, +)

Figure 4.4. Children that can do some (maybe even all) of the items shown above are showing a readiness for kindergarten! Congratulations, you have laid the foundation for future success. Sit back and watch your child soar!

children to language, the most important building block for future reading success. Hearing more words helps to develop a larger vocabulary. A larger vocabulary leads to good reading skills.

There is no need to worry if your young child (under the age of six) does not show signs of an interest in reading. But do see your child's pediatrician as soon as possible if you have concerns about their language development, hearing, or sight. Learning is a life-long journey, not a quick weekend getaway. When you make print and reading a regular part of your young child's life, learning will occur naturally. Did you ever imagine that something so enjoyable for *both* you and your baby could result in so many future educational benefits?

NOTE

1. E. Sulzby, "Children's Emergent Reading of Favorite Storybooks: A Developmental Study," *Reading Research Quarterly* (1985): 458–481.

Chapter Five

For Tech-Savvy Adults

While the American Academy of Pediatrics (AAP) recommends no television (or screen media such as computer games, videos, or DVDs) for children under two, it is unrealistic for us to ignore the magnitude of resources that surround us. The tools discussed in this chapter are always best accessed with a critical eye, keeping in mind that although children may learn some concepts from educational technology, they learn best from interactive, hands-on experiences with people they care about. The resources below are intended to guide caregivers in their journey to prepare their own children for their journey to kindergarten. As in all parenting decisions, common sense is the best guide.

EARLY LITERACY RESOURCES FOR ADULTS

Websites

Get Ready to Read! is for educators and parents of young children interested in the development of early literacy skills in the years before kindergarten. The site is a service of the National Center for Learning Disabilities. The resources and information provided on this site promote skill building, communication between adults, and ways to address concerns. Under the "Early Literacy" tab, topics such as "Getting the Most Out of Picture Books," "Quality Television Shows That Focus on Early Literacy," "Get Ready to Read! Literacy Checklists," and "When Parents Are Concerned About Their Child's Early Learning Skills" are innovative. www.getreadytoread.org

Get Set for K is a part of the Charlotte Mecklenburg Library's website. The month-by-month guide to school readiness offers parents and caregivers an

early literacy skill to focus on for each month of the year. Then, they offer activity suggestions easy enough for every family to implement. While some suggestions are more appropriate for children in preschool, many can be used with babies and toddlers.
www.cmlibrary.org/kids/getset4k

Reach Out and Read is a nonprofit organization with a goal of promoting early literacy and school readiness. They focus on the medical field's involvement of giving new books to children when they visit their doctor's office. Through physician guidance, they advocate for the importance of reading aloud. Resources that can be found on their website and used by all parents include book suggestions, typical literacy milestones, and recordings of classic children's books that can be streamed through the website.
www.reachoutandread.org

Reading Rockets is a national literacy initiative that offers information and resources on how young kids learn to read, why so many struggle, and how caring adults can help. Under the "Early Literacy Development" topic, visitors to the site can watch videos about literacy development, find activities to use with young children, explore the latest research on parent involvement in education, and much, much more. Literacy milestones from birth to age three are offered.
www.readingrockets.org/atoz/early_literacy_development/

Caroline Jackson Blakemore and Barbara Weston Ramirez, the authors of the website Read to Your Baby, are reading specialists. Together they have over fifty years of experience helping elementary school children with reading difficulties. They instruct new parents in the field of emergent literacy and offer practical suggestions on how babies and toddlers will best achieve future school success. Specifically, they offer wonderful read-aloud tips, resources, and up-to-date research about babies and toddlers and their acquisition of language and literacy development.
www.Readtoyourbaby.com

Reading Is Fundamental (RIF) is the largest children's literacy nonprofit in the United States. The organization delivers free books and literacy resources to families who need them the most. RIF provides new, free books for children to choose from and make their own. According to RIF, by being provided with books, the children are empowered and motivated to see new possibilities. Highlights from their website include the following:

- An "Activities" section offers learning opportunities for every age group and skill level through cultural, dramatic, and writing activities.
- "Booklists" provide book suggestions by topic, ranging from award winners to multicultural suggestions.
- The "Articles" section is full of ideas for teachers and parents wishing to encourage reading in new ways.
- The "Brochures" are easy-to-read guides offering tips for reading with young children and tips for selecting age-appropriate books for youngsters.

www.rif.org

Rocky Mountain Public Broadcasting Services and Colorado Libraries for Early Literacy present <u>Storyblocks</u>. Storyblocks is a collection of thirty- to sixty-second videos which model for parents and caregivers songs, rhymes, and fingerplays appropriate for early childhood.
www.storyblocks.org

Jim Trelease is the author of the million-copy bestseller, *The Read-Aloud Handbook*. Mr. Trelease has traveled to all fifty states and abroad, advocating the benefits of reading aloud to children. He has been recognized by both teachers and parents for his message that books are friends, not enemies. Sixty U.S. colleges use his *Handbook* as a text for education students. The useful website is chock-full of information related to literacy. From discussions about reading education to booklists to research regarding the effects of television, Mr. Trelease's website covers it all. Free brochures and slides from his lectures are available for printing. Weekly read-aloud book reviews and a weekly essay from the author on current reading issues keep the site remarkably current.
www.trelease-on-reading.com

Zero to Three is a nonprofit organization intent on informing, training, and supporting adults who are working to improve the lives of infants and toddlers. Their specific mission is to "promote the health and development of infants and toddlers." Their site is full of development charts, tips, and tools about child development and tips regarding age-appropriate play. The site also offers information about school readiness, early literacy, and language development.
www.zerotothree.org

Read more at the author of this title's own website: http://www.dawn-roginski.com

Television

Many preschool children enjoy TV, and some shows have more potential than others. Keep in mind that young children often imitate what they see, good or bad. Think about your child's age and choose the types of things that you want him to see, learn, and imitate.

When choosing the programs that are appropriate for your child, the best children's programming must

- teach your child something,
- hold his interest,
- encourage him to listen and question,
- help him expand his vocabulary,
- make him feel good about himself, and
- introduce him to new ideas and things.

Some additional tips to help guide your decisions about television:

- Limit the time that you allow your child to watch TV. Too much television cuts into important activities in a child's life, such as reading, playing, and talking.
- Always watch TV with your child, conversing with him about what he is seeing and hearing. Answer questions and point out how the program relates to your child's everyday life.
- Go to the library and find books that explore the themes of the TV shows that your child watches. Or, help your child to use his own drawing ability to make a picture or book based on a TV show that is enjoyed.

A sample of quality television shows that incorporate early skills include the following:

64 Zoo Lane is an animated series developed to introduce children to new vocabulary and foster a love of language through interesting characters and storytelling. Developed for children from ages four to six, this program provides children and adults with many opportunities to explore how language is used and uses problem-solving techniques to explore new vocabulary. Each thirty-minute episode takes the viewers along as the main character, Lucy, visits her neighborhood zoo after hours, when all the animals are eager to share their stories.

Between the Lions was developed by the makers of Sesame Street. *Between the Lions* is designed to foster literacy skills in children between the ages of four and seven. Based on a family of lions who live in a library, this show gives children many of the experiences they need to be successful readers when they enter school. *Between the Lions* is broadcast through your local PBS station.

Maisy is a welcoming, preschool-aged mouse. Based on the books by Lucy Cousins, this thirty-minute program introduces children to story structure, builds an appreciation for language, and finds ways to explore the alphabet. Developed for children between the ages of four and six, this program contains a lively cast of animal friends that *Maisy* interacts with as she explores her world. *Maisy* episodes can be viewed online by visiting www.maisyfun. com or through Lucy Cousin's website.

Mr. Rogers' Neighborhood debuted in 1967 as a new type of television show for children between the ages of two and five. This show teaches young children about themselves and the world around them by introducing them to real people and make-believe characters. Through these stories and experiences, children learn fundamental skills they will need to become readers. *Mr. Rogers' Neighborhood* promotes skills like listening, understanding the beginning, middle, and end of a story, as well as predicting what will happen next. Each episode is thirty minutes in length and is connected to a weekly theme. *Mr. Rogers' Neighborhood* is broadcast through PBS stations across the country.

Reading Rainbow promotes the love of books and reading and serves to encourage positive reading attitudes. Developed for children between the ages of four and eight, *Reading Rainbow* remains a favorite with teachers because of the mixed social and cultural topics. Each thirty-minute show hosted by LeVar Burton includes segments such as a story read by guest readers, recommendations for books to read by other young children, and interviews with children on a wide range of issues. *Reading Rainbow* is broadcast through PBS stations across the country.

Sesame Street, originally designed in 1968, was designed to help children transition from home to school by introducing the alphabet and numbers through interesting characters, songs, and stories. This sixty-minute show is backed by a curriculum grounded in years of research and continuous work with educational experts. Through this work with teachers, researchers, and parents, *Sesame Street* continues to evolve, growing with the needs of today's children and their caregivers. *Sesame Street* is broadcast through PBS stations.

Computers

Children as young as three years old, though they can't read yet, may enjoy exploring some computer websites with a caring adult. When you are sitting in front of a computer with your child, join in at first and watch as he plays. Make sure that you choose the right programs for your child's age. There are many computer programs available for children, but they vary in quality so it is wise to try it yourself before exposing it to your child. While many television shows advertise related websites, not all cater to building early literacy skills and are more interested in marketing their products. However, all of the shows listed above *do* offer early literacy activities that might interest your child and continue their interest in developing early literacy skills. Type the show's name into your favorite web browser to try them.

TumbleBooks is an online collection of favorite previously published picture books that have been enhanced with animation, sounds, and narration. You can read, or have the story read to your child. While this is a subscription-based resource, many public libraries have subscriptions to *TumbleBooks*, and it can be accessed through your local library's website (you may need to have your library card to enter depending on the set-up of your local library's site). You can visit the *TumbleBooks* website for information on purchasing a private subscription.

StoryPlace was originally developed with support and contributions from Smart Start of Mecklenburg County. The 2015 redesign was supported by grant funds from the Institute of Museum and Library Services under the provisions of the federal Library Services and Technology Act. *StoryPlace* came about to provide children with the virtual experience of going to the library and participating in the same types of activities the library offers in its physical locations. The site also includes early literacy information for parents and caregivers.

Apps for Your Devices

Apps are potential tools for learning, but how you and your child use the app together determines how rich of a learning experience it is. The more your child is encouraged to experiment, problem-solve, and think, the more learning will take place. Be sure that content is developmentally appropriate. It should reflect your child's experiences in the real world, such as exploring the zoo, learning about animals, or helping your child see that in the virtual zoo on the screen, the purple cage door is opened with the matching purple key. Any digital device being used by a young child is best used with an adult who is engaging the child in continual conversation and guiding the digital experience. Guided play means asking questions that help problem-solve. For example, when a child is struggling with a puzzle app, you might ask, "Should we start with the straight lined edges or the corners which have two straight sides?" or "What if we turn this piece upside down, will it fit then?" Guide your child with words rather than "doing it" for them.

Examples of some age-appropriate, interactive apps are given below:

Animatch is an electronic matching game that features farm and safari animal cards to flip and match as in a card memory game. When children succeed at a match, they hear animal sounds and see the animals do a jig.

JumpStart Preschool Magic of Learning is hosted by Frankie the Dog who takes children on a learning adventure through four types of games. *Bug Catcher* focuses on color, shape, and number recognition; *Present Search* requires children to listen closely and follow instructions; *Matching Duckies* develops memory; and *Barnyard Fun* helps children identify upper-case and lowercase letters. JumpStart computer games were released in 1994 for all age levels. They continue to be updated with interactive learning experiences for children and can be purchased at most electronic stores.

Peg + Cat Big Gig. Through singing, Peg and Cat will help your child identify numbers, count up and down by ones and twos, and repeat patterns. Kids are rewarded with a special show when they complete each challenge.

TeachMe: Kindergarten allows a grown-up to introduce their child to basic math, reading, and spelling concepts. You can select individual activities such as sight words, numbers, addition, subtraction, letters, and spelling. Additionally, the adult can set different difficulty levels. Participants earn coins for correct answers, and the rewards can be used to buy virtual stickers to place onto backdrops or to buy fish in order to create an online aquarium. *TeachMe: Toddler* is also available.

YouTube Videos

Videos online can be accessed by using a variety of keywords. However, the search results may not also be appropriate for children. Always seek out the videos you plan to use with your child prior to sitting them in front of the screen.

From https://jbrary.com, you can find Dana and Lindsey, two children's librarians from Vancouver, British Columbia, who offer a wealth of story time information. Most impressive is their collection of YouTube videos performing finger plays, nursery rhymes, flannel board activities, and so much more! Join them to learn all sorts of songs, rhymes, fingerplays, and more by visiting https://jbrary.com/youtube-playlists/.

Kids TV, at https://www.youtube.com/channel/UC7Pq3Ko42YpkCB_ Q4E98ljw, offers compilations of 3D animated kids' rhymes and educational videos. Together, you can introduce your toddler to a variety of English rhymes, baby songs, and nursery rhymes such as "Humpty Dumpty," "The Incy Wincy Spider," "The ABC Song," and a variety of 1-2-3 songs. Bob the Train explores the alphabet, numbers, colors, and shapes.

To learn more about the impact of screen use with young children and how to make informed digital choices for your child, visit Common Sense Media at www.commonsensemedia.org.

Most importantly, always keep in mind that *you*, not an electronic device, make the difference in your child's learning. Technology, in moderation, can be a tool to reinforce the activities you and your child have already discovered together: talking, singing, reading, playing, and writing.

For caregivers who wish to learn more about early literacy and to be connected with additional resources, appendix D recommends wonderful websites for more information.

Appendix A

Rhyme and Lap Jogs for Babies

Babies love to hear the sound of their caregiver's voice. They love to hear rhymes and watch your mouth as you sing or chant to them. Many of the rhymes have actions to accompany them. Before attempting any bouncing motions, be sure your baby's head and neck are strong enough for the motion. If you are unsure, it is perfectly fine to use the rhymes without the activities. Also consider your baby's temperament before trying any rhyme. Some babies love to be roughly bounced and do not want their grown-ups to ever stop jostling them. (Be mindful of the baby's last feeding—too much bouncing may bring the meal up unexpectedly!) Other babies may prefer softer and gentler actions. Feel free to adapt the rhymes and movement to your particular baby. No one way is the "correct" way to share a rhyme with your child.

APPLESAUCE

Criss cross applesauce
(mark an "x" on the baby's back or belly)
Spiders crawling up your spine
(creep your fingers up the baby's back or belly)
Cool breeze
(blow on the baby's ear)
Tight squeeze
(hug the baby)
Now you've got the shivers

BABY GROWS

Five little fingers on this hand
Five little fingers on that
A dear little nose
A mouth like a rose
Two rosy cheeks that glow
Two eyes, two ears
And ten little toes
Watch the baby every day
To see how fast he grows
(lightly touch or tickle each part of the baby as you recite the rhyme)

THE BABY IN THE CRADLE

The baby in the cradle goes rock, rock, rock
(rock arms as if holding an infant)
The clock on the dresser goes tick, tock, tock
(shake pointer finger back and forth)
The rain on the window goes pat, pat, pat
(tap fingers together)
Out comes the sun
So we clap, clap, clap
(clap the baby's hands together)

BLOW THE FIRE

Jeremiah blow the fire puff, puff, puff
First you blow it gently
(blow on each of the baby's ear)
Then you blow it rough
(tickle behind the baby's ear)

BOUNCE ME

Bounce me, bounce me on your knee
Bounce me, bounce me pretty please
Bounce me, bounce me here and there

Bounce me, bounce me everywhere
(bounce the baby on your lap, shifting the baby's weight from one leg to the other)

BOUNCING, BOUNCING ON MY KNEE

Bouncing, bouncing on my knee
Bouncing, bouncing on my knee
Bouncing, bouncing on my knee
Just Baby and me
(bounce the baby on knees)
I'll swing you high and swing you low
(lift the baby up and down)
I'll hold you close, and I won't let go
(hug the baby)

CHEEK CHIN

Cheek, chin, cheek, chin
(touch the baby as you say the rhyme)
Cheek, chin, NOSE
Cheek, chin, cheek, chin
Cheek, chin, TOES
Cheek, chin, cheek, chin
Cheek, chin, UP BABY GOES
(lift the baby up)

COBBLER, COBBLER

Cobbler, cobbler, mend my shoe
Get it done by half past two
Half past two is much too late
Get it done by half past eight
(tap the rhythm on the baby's feet, alternating)

DAVY, DAVY DUMPLING

Davy, Davy Dumpling
Boil him in a pot

(bounce the baby in your lap)
Sugar him
(tickle the baby's belly)
Butter him
(tickle the baby's ears)
Eat him while he's hot
(kiss the baby's ears or belly)

DIDDLE DIDDLE DUMPLING

Diddle, diddle, dumpling, my son John
Went to bed with his stockings on
(lay the baby on their back and bicycle their legs)
One shoe off, and one shoe on
(tap bottom of the baby's feet, alternating)
Diddle, diddle, dumpling, my son John
(bicycle the baby's legs)

FEE-FIE-FOE-FUM

Fee, fie, foe, fum
(walk your fingers up the baby's body)
See my fingers
(show the baby your hand)
See my thumb
(show the baby your thumb)
Fee, fie, foe, fum
(walk your fingers down the baby's body)
Fingers gone
(hide your hand behind you)
So is thumb

GIDDY-UP

Come and climb on Mommy's knee
Take a horsey ride with me
Giddy-up giddy-up
Ride to town

(bounce the baby on your lap)
Giddy-up, giddy-up
Up and down
(lower your knees with the baby sitting on them)
Giddy-up fast and giddy-up slow
Giddy-up, giddy-up, Whoa!
(bounce the baby fast and then slow)

HICKORY DICKORY DOCK

Hickoy Dickory dock
The mouse ran up the clock
(move the baby from side to side as they sit on your lap
The clock struck one
The mouse ran down
Hickory dickory dock
(run your fingers up and down the baby's arm)

HANKY PANKY

Down by the banks of the hanky panky
(bounce the baby on your knees)
Where the bullfrogs jump from bank to banky
(move the baby's weight from side to side on your lap)
They went oops, opps, belly flops
(lift the baby up and down twice)
One missed the lily pad and went kerplops
(bounce the baby again and lift their bottom up into the air)

HIPPETY-HOP

Hippety hop to the bakery shop
To buy three sticks of candy
One for you
One for me
And one for sister Sandy
(bounce the baby to the rhythm on your lap)

HOT CROSS BUNS

Hot cross buns
Hot cross buns
One a-penny, two a-penny
Hot cross buns
(clap out the rhythm with the baby's hands or on the bottom of the baby's feet)

ICKY, BICKY, SODA CRACKER

Icky, bicky, soda cracker
(Bounce to the rhythm)
Icky, bicky, boo
(lean forward on "boo")
Icky, bicky, soda cracker
(bounce to the rhythm)
Up goes you
(lift the baby up)

THE ITSY BITSY SPIDER

The itsy bitsy spider
Climbed up the waterspout
Down came the rain
And washed the spider out
Out came the sun
And dried up all the rain
So the itsy bitsy spider
Climbed up the spout again
(walk your fingers all over the baby so as to tickle them)

JACK BE NIMBLE

Jack be nimble
Jack be quick
(bounce the baby on your knees)
Jack jump over
The candlestick
(lift the baby up)

JACK-IN-THE-BOX

Jack, jack, down you go
Down in your box, down so low
(cover the baby's eyes)
Jack, Jack, there goes your top
Quickly now, up you pop!
(uncover the baby's eyes)

KISSY GAME

Kissy, kissy fingers
Kissy, kissy toes
Kissy, kissy baby
On your kissy nose
I love to kiss your fingers
I love to kiss your nose
I love to kiss my baby
On her kissy nose
(kiss or tickle corresponding parts of the baby)

KISSING RHYME

Up, up in the sky like this
(lift the baby up over your head)
Down, down for a great big kiss
(lower the baby down)
Up like this
(lift the baby up)
Down for a kiss
(lower the baby and kiss)
You're a special baby
(hug the baby)

LEG OVER LEG

Leg over leg
As the dog went to Dover
When he came to a stile

(bounce the baby on your lap)
Jump!
(lift the baby up)
He went over
(return the baby to your lap)

LITTLE PONY

Ride a little pony
Down to town
Better be careful
(bounce the baby on your lap)
You don't fall down
(tip the baby backward away from you)

MIX A PANCAKE

Mix a pancake
Stir a pancake
(turn the baby's arms as if stirring a bowl)
Pop it in the pan
(bounce the baby one time)
Fry the pancake
(bounce baby on your knees quickly)
Toss the pancake
(lift the baby)
Catch it if you can
(give the baby hug)

MOTHER AND FATHER AND UNCLE JOHN

Mother and Father and Uncle John
(the baby on your knees)
Went to town one by one
(bounce the baby on your knees)
Father fell off
(lean the baby to one side)

Mother fell off
(lean the baby to the other side)
But Uncle John rode on and on
(bounce)
Father fell off
(lean to one side)
Mother fell off
(lean to the other side)
But Uncle John rode on and on and on
(bounce faster)

THE NOBLE DUKE OF YORK

Oh, the noble Duke of York
He had ten thousand men
He marched them up to the top of the hill
(bounce the baby up on your lap)
And marched them down again
(bounce the baby down on your lap)
And when they're up, they're up
(raise knees up)
And when they're down, they're down
(lower knees)
And when they're only halfway up
(raise knees halfway up)
They're neither up nor down
(quickly raise up and down)
Oh, the noble Duke of York
He had ten thousand men
He marched them up to the top of the hill
And marched them down again
(bounce the baby down on your lap)
He marched them to the left
(gently tip the baby to left)
He marched them to the right
(gently tip the baby to right)
He even marched them upside down
(roll the baby onto chest as you roll backward)
Oh, what a silly sight

Appendix A

THE OLD GREY CAT IS SLEEPING

The old grey cat is sleeping, sleeping, sleeping
The old grey cat is sleeping in the house
The little mice are creeping, creeping, creeping
The little mice are creeping in the house
(slowly walk fingers up and down the baby's arms and legs)
The old grey cat is creeping, creeping, creeping
The old grey cat is creeping in the house
The little mice go scampering, scampering, scampering
The little mice go scampering in the house
(quickly walk fingers up and down the baby's arms and legs)

ONE LITTLE BABY

One little baby rocking in a tree.
(rock arms)
Two little babies splashing in the sea.
(pretend to splash)
Three little babies crawling on the floor.
(crawl fingers on the knee)
Four little babies banging on the door.
(pretend to knock)
Five little babies playing hide and seek.
(cover your eyes)
Keep your eyes closed now . . . until I say . . . PEEK!
(uncover eyes)

PAT-A-CAKE

Pat-a-cake, pat-a-cake, baker's man
Bake me a cake as fast as you can
Roll it and pat it and mark it with a 'B'
And put it in the oven for baby and me
(clap the baby's hands to rhythm and tickle belly)

PEASE PORRIDGE HOT

Pease porridge hot
Pease porridge cold

Pease porridge in the pot
Nine days old
Some like it hot
Some like it cold
Some like it in the pot
Nine days old
(clap the baby's hands or tap the rhythm on the bottom of the baby's feet)

PEEK-A-BOO

Baby's gone, where is she?
(cover the baby's eyes)
Peek-a-boo, now I see
(uncover the baby's eyes)
Gone again?
(cover the baby's eyes)
Where'd he go?
Peek-A-Boo
(uncover eyes)
I found her toe!
(softly tug the baby's toe)

PIZZA, PICKLE, PUMPERNICKEL

Pizza, pickle, pumpernickel
My little baby shall have a tickle
(walk your fingers along the baby's belly)
One for her fingers
(tickle the baby's fingers)
One for his toes
(tickle the baby's toes)
One for her belly
Where the (cereal) goes
(tickle the baby's belly)

PONY BOY (OR GIRL)

Pony boy, pony boy
Won't you be my pony boy
Don't say "No"

Here we go
Giddy-up, giddy-up
(bounce the baby on your knees progressively faster)
Whoa!

RICKETY, RICKETY ROCKING HORSE

Rickety, rickety, rocking horse
Over the fields we go
Rickety, rickety, rocking horse
Gitty up! Gitty up!
(bounce the baby to the rhythm)
Whoa!
(roll backward, the baby onto your chest)

ROBBIE THE RABBIT

Robbie the rabbit is fat, fat, fat
(tap the baby's belly)
His soft little paws go pat, pat, pat
(tap the baby's feet)
His soft little ears go flop, flop, flop
(tap the baby's ears)
When Robbie runs he goes hop, hop, hop
(bounce the baby three times)

ROUND ABOUT THERE

Round about there
Sat a little hare
A cat came to chase him
(walk your fingers up and down the baby's arms)
Right up there
(tickle the baby under their chin)

ROUND AND ROUND THE GARDEN

Round and round the garden, like a Teddy Bear
(gently trace finger in a circle around child's palm)

One step, two step
(walk fingers up child's arm)
Tickle you under there
(tickle under chin, under arm, or tummy)

SHOE THE OLD HORSE

Shoe the old horse
Shoe the old mare
(tap bottom of the baby's feet)
But let the little pony run
Bare, bare, bare
(bicycle the baby's legs for them)

SLOWLY, VERY SLOWLY

Slowly, slowly, very slowly
(Walk fingers up the baby's arm slowly)
Creeps the garden snail
Slowly, slowly, very slowly
Up the wooden rail
Quickly, quickly, very quickly,
(Run fingers up the arm quickly)
Runs the little mouse
Quickly, quickly, very quickly
Round about the house

TEN LITTLE HORSES

Ten little horses galloped into town
(Gallop the baby on your knees.)
Five were black and five were brown
(Emphasize one hand, then the other.)
They galloped up
(Gallop the baby up.)
They galloped down
(Gallop the baby down.)
Then they galloped out of town
(Gallop knees quickly.)

THESE ARE BABY'S FINGERS

These are Baby's fingers
(Tickle fingers)
These are Baby's toes
(Tickle toes)
This is Baby's tummy button
(Tickle belly)
Round and round it goes.

THIS IS THE WAY THE LADIES RIDE

This is the way the ladies ride
Walk, walk, walk
(Bounce gently)
This is the way the gentlemen ride
Trot trot trot.
(Bounce slightly more)
This is the way the children ride
Gallopy-trot, gallopy-trot
Gallopy, gallopy, gallopy, gallopy
All fall off
(Bounce more and more, then capture the child in your arms as she "falls" off.)

THIS LITTLE PIGGY

This little piggy went to market
This little piggy stayed at home
This little piggy had roast beef
This little piggy had none
And this little piggy went
"Wee wee wee" all the way home
(wiggle each toe in turn)

TOES

Big toe
Tall toe
Middle toe strong

Funny Toe
Little toe
(tug each toe as it is named)
Bongity, bong, bong
(bounce the baby or tap the bottom of their feet three times)

TO MARKET, TO MARKET

To market, to market, to buy a fat pig
(Bounce the baby on your knees, alternating speed)
Home again, home again, dancing a jig
To market, to market, to buy a fat hog
Home again, home again, jiggety-jog
To market, to market, to buy a plum bun
Home again, home again, market is done

TWO LITTLE BLACKBIRDS

Two little blackbirds sitting on a hill
One named Jack and one named Jill
(show the baby your left, then right hand)
Fly away Jack
(hide your right hand)
Fly away Jill
(hide your left hand)
Come back Jack
(return your right hand and show the baby)
Come back Jill
(return your left hand and show the baby)

UP IN THE SKY

Up, up, up in the sky like this
(Gently lift the baby in the air)
Down, down for a great big kiss
(Slowly bring the baby down and kiss)
Up like this
(Lift up)
Down for a kiss

(Lower down)
You're a special baby
(Hug and cuddle the baby)

WHERE IS THUMBKIN

Where is Thumbkin
Where is Thumbkin
Here I am
(show the baby right thumb)
Here I am
(show the baby left thumb)
"How are you today sir?"
(have right thumb wiggle to the left thumb)
"Very well I thank you"
(have left thumb wiggle to the right thumb)
Run away
(hide right hand)
Run away
(hide left hand)

Appendix B

Baby and Toddler Discography

Barney's Greatest Hits: The Early Years. Capitol Records, 2000. Sound Recording.

Bartels, Joanie. *Morning Magic.* Van Nuys, CA: BMG Music, 1987. Sound Recording.

Buchman, Rachel. *Sing a Song of Seasons.* Cambridge, MA: Rounder Kids, 1997. Sound Recording.

Cedarmont Kid Singers. *100 Sing-Along-Songs For Kids.* Franklin, TN: 2007. Sound Recording.

A Child's Celebration of Song. Redway, CA: Music for Little People, 1992. Sound Recording.

Darby, Kara. *Sing & Move.* Starkville, MS: Munchkin Musik Makers Productions, 2011. Sound Recording.

Diaper Gym: (Fun Activities for Babies on the Move). Long Branch, NJ: Kimbo Educational, 1985. Sound Recording.

Dines, Katherine. *Hunk-ta-bunk-ta wiggle. Volume One: 12 Tunes for Toddlers.* Denver, CO: Hunk-Ta-Bunk-Ta Music, 2006. Sound Recording.

Downing, Johnette. *Music Time.* New Orleans, LA: Wiggle Worm Records, 2005. Sound Recording.

Feierabend, John Martin. *Frog in the Meadow: (Music, Now I'm Two).* Chicago, IL: GIA Publications, 2000. Sound Recording.

———. *Ride Away on Your Horses: (Music, Now I'm One!)* Chicago, IL: GIA Publications, 2000. Sound Recording.

Fletcher, Dave. *All of Two of Us.* CD Baby, 2012. http://www.cdbaby.com/cd/musicformoving

Gil, Jim. *Jim Gill Sings the Sneezing Song and Other Contagious Tunes.* Oak Park, IL: Jim GillMusic, 2013. Sound Recording.

Hammett, Carol Totsky. *It's Toddler Time.* Long Branch, NJ: Kimbo Educational 1982. Sound Recording.

———. *Preschool Action Time: Activities and Finger Plays.* Long Branch, NJ: Kimbo Educational, 1988.

————. *Toddlers on Parade: [Musical Exercises for Infants and Toddlers].* Long Branch, NJ: Kimbo Educational, 1988.

Hegner, Priscilla A. *Baby Games.* Long Branch, NJ: Kimbo Educational, 1987. Sound Recording.

Learning Station. *Kids Nursery Rhymes. Volume 1.* US: Master Song, 2001. Sound Recording.

————. *Get Funky and Musical Fun with the Learning Station.* Melbourne, FL: Learning Station, 2003. Sound Recording.

————. *Teach a Toddler: Playful Songs for Learning.* Long Branch, NJ: Kimbo Educational, 1985. Sound Recording.

McGrath, Bob. *Sing Along with Bob #1.* Teaneck, NJ: Bob's Kids Music, 2000. Sound Recording.

More Silly Songs. Burbank, CA: Walt Disney Records, 1998. Sound Recording.

Music for Moving. *Preschool Action Songs 2 (Ages 3–7); Pre–K & Kindergarten Music for YoungChildren,* 2013. http://www.cdbaby.com/cd/musicformoving.

Palmer, Hap. *Peek-A-Boo: and Other Songs for Young Children.* Topanga, CA: Hap-Pal Music, 1997. Sound Recording.

————. *Two Little Sounds: Fun with Phonics and Numbers.* Topanga, CA: Hap-Pal Music, 2003. Sound Recording.

————. *Walter the Waltzing Worm.* Freeport, NY: Activity Records, Inc, 1982. Sound Recording.

Peterson, Carole. *Dancing Feet.* [United States]: Macaroni Soup, 2008. Sound Recording.

————. *H.U.M. All Year Long: Highly Usable Music Kids Can Sing, Dance & Do.* [United States]: Macaroni Soup, 2003. Sound Recording.

————. *Season Sings!* [United States]: Macaroni Soup, 2012. Sound Recording.

————. *Sticky Bubble Gum and Other Tasty Tunes: Sing Along, Dance Along, Do Along.* [United States]: Macaroni Soup, 2003. Sound Recording.

Piggyback Songs: Singable Poems Set to Favorite Tunes. Long Branch, NJ: Kimbo, 1995. Sound Recording.

Raffi. *One Light, One Sun.* Willowdale, ON: Shoreline Records; Cambridge, MA: Distributed by Rounder Records [1996], 1985. Sound Recording.

Sloane, Shari. *Singing with Shari: Oldies but Goodies.* 2013. http://www.cdbaby.com/cd/sharisloane3.

Stewart, Georgiana Liccione. *Action Songs for Preschoolers: a Treasury of Fun.* LongBranch, NJ: Kimbo Educational, 2003. Sound Recording.

————. *Baby Face.* Long Branch, NJ: Kimbo Educational, 1983. Sound Recording.

Sunseri, MaryLee. *Baby-O!* Pacific Grove, CA: Piper Grove Music, 2005. Sound Recording.

Valeri, Michele. *Little Ditties for Itty Bitties.* [S.l.]: Community Music, 2010. Sound Recording.

Wiggles. *Racing to the Rainbow.* New York: Koch Records, 2007. Sound Recording.

Wonder Kids Choir. *Favorite Sing-A-Longs. Volumes 1–3.* St. Laurent, Quebec, Canada: Madacy Entertainment Group, Inc., 2000. Sound Recording.

Appendix C

100 Picture Books to Know
Before Kindergarten

These are just guides as to whom each title is best suited. However, children enjoy different books at different times. There is no right or wrong time to try a title with a child. Go back to old favorites as children age. Try books that didn't interest a young child at an older age. Perhaps their interests have changed and the old title will now be of great interest.

Author	Title	Best for*	Synopsis
Allard, Harry	Miss Nelson is Missing!	P	Miss Nelson comes up missing and o the horror of her class an evil substitute arrives named Miss Viola Swamp!
Asch, Frank	Happy Birthday, Moon	T	Bear climbs a mountain to find out when the moon's birthday is so that he can buy the moon a birthday present.
Baker, Keith	Big Fat Hen	B	Big Fat Hen counts to ten with her friends and all her chicks.
Bang, Molly	Ten, Nine, Eight	B	A father and his little girl count down objects from ten to one as she prepares to go to bed.
Barrett, Judi	Cloudy With A Chance of Meatballs	P	In the town of Chewandswallow it rains soup and juice, snows mashed potatoes, and blows storms of hamburgers—until the weather changes.

Author	Title	Best for*	Synopsis
Barton, Byron	The Little Red Hen	T	None of the little red hen's lazy friends are willing to help her plant, harvest, or grind wheat into flour, but all are eager to eat the bread she makes from it.
Behmelmans, Ludwig	Madeline	P	In an orphanage in Paris, brave Madeline's is taken to the hospital after she comes down with appendicitis.
Bingham, Kelly.	Z is for Moose	P	Moose is eager to play his part in the alphabet book but is disappointed when his letter passes. Even though he behaves badly, Zebra finds a spot for him.
Brett, Jan	The Mitten: A Ukrainian Folktale	P	A boy's lost mitten is discovered by a group of curious woodland animals.
Brown, Marcia	Stone Soup: an Old Tale	P	Three hungry soldiers trick French villagers into sharing their food with them by concocting a wonderful pot of stone soup.
Brown, Margaret Wise	Goodnight Moon	B	A little bunny bids goodnight to all the objects in his room before falling asleep.
Brunhoff, Jean de	The Story of Babar, the Little Elephant	P	An orphaned baby elephant goes to live in the city with an old lady who gives him everything he wants, but he returns to the forest where he is crowned king of the elephants.
Burningham, John	Mr. Gumpy's Outing	P	Mr. Gumpy accepts more and more riders on his boat until the inevitable occurs.
Burton, Virginia Lee	Mike Mulligan and His Steam Shovel: Story and Pictures	P	Although threatened by competition from modern shovels, Mike proves the worth of his old steam shovel.
Campbell, Rod	Dear Zoo	T	The zoo sends a bunch of possible pets but all fail to suit its prospective owner.

Author	Title	Best for*	Synopsis
Carle, Eric	The Very Hungry Caterpillar	B	A hungry caterpillar eats his way through a large quantity of food until he forms a cocoon around himself and goes to sleep.
Cooney, Barbara	Miss Rumphius	P	As a child Great-Aunt Alice Rumphius resolved that when she grew up she would go to faraway places, live by the sea in her old age, and do something to make the world more beautiful.
Crews, Donald	Freight Train	T	A colorful train goes through tunnels, by cities, and over trestles.
Cronin, Doreen	Click, Clack, Moo: Cows that Type	P	Farmer Brown's cows find a typewriter in the barn and start making demands on the farmer who refuses to give them what they want.
DePaola, Tomie	Strega Nona: an Old Tale	P	Strega Nona leaves Big Anthony alone with her magic pasta pot, who is determined to show the townspeople how it works.
Eastman, P.D.	Are You My Mother?	P	Never having seen his mother, a baby bird makes mistakes as he tries to find her.
Ehlert, Lois	Growing Vegetable Soup	T	A father and child grow vegetables and make them into a soup.
Emberley, Ed	Go Away, Big Green Monster	T	A scary green monster begins to disappear, page by page, as the reader commands it.
Falconer, Ian	Olivia	P	Olivia is a pig who has too much energy for her own good.
Feiffer, Jules	Bark, George	T	George does not sound like a puppy and his mother takes him to the veterinarian.
Fleming, Denise	Lunch	B	A very hungry mouse eats a large lunch comprised of colorful foods.

Author	Title	Best for*	Synopsis
Freeman, Don	Corduroy	P	A toy bear in a department store wants a number of things, but when a little girl finally buys him he finds what he has always wanted most of all.
Gag, Wanda	Millions of Cats	P	An old man makes an unwise decision when he brings too many cats home to his wife.
Galdone, Paul	The Three Billy Goats Gruff	P	Colorful illustrations accompany this version of the classic children's tale of three goat brothers and a contemptible troll.
Guarina, Deborah	Is Your Mama a Llama?	T	A young llama asks his friends if their mamas are llamas and finds out, that their mothers are other types of animals.
Henkes, Kevin	Chrysanthemum	P	Chrysanthemum thinks her name is absolutely perfect, until the kids at school make fun of her.
Henkes, Kevin	Lilly's Purple Plastic Purse	P	Lilly loves her teacher, but when he asks her to wait a while before showing her new purse, she does something for which she is sorry later.
Hill, Eric	Where's Spot?	B	A mother dog finds eight other animals hiding around the house before finding her lost puppy.
Hoban, Russell	Bread and Jam for Frances	P	Frances decides she likes to eat only bread and jam at every meal, until her parents grant her wish.
Hoffman, Mary	Amazing Grace	P	Grace wants the lead in Peter Pan, but he wasn't black and Grace is. But Grace proves you can be anything you want.
Hutchins, Pat	Rosie's Walk	T	Rosie is followed around the farm by a hen and a fox.
Johnson, Crockett	Harold and the Purple Crayon	P	Harold draws himself into an adventure with his purple crayon.

Author	Title	Best for*	Synopsis
Kasza, Keiko	The Wolf's Chicken Stew	P	A hungry wolf's tries to fatten a chicken for his stew.
Keats, Ezra Jack	The Snowy Day	P	Peter is delighted with the deep snow and plays outdoors all day.
Kimmel, Eric	Anansi and the Moss Covered Rock	P	Anansi the Spider uses a strange moss-covered rock in the forest to trick all the other animals, until Deer decides to teach him a lesson.
Kraus, Ruth	The Carrot Seed	P	A little boy plants and cares for a carrot seed even though others tell him that nothing will grow.
Leaf, Munro	The Story of Ferdinand	P	A gentle Spanish bull would rather smell flowers than fight.
Lionni, Leo	Swimmy	P	A little black fish in a school of red fish finds a way to protect them all from their natural enemies.
Litwin, Eric	Pete the Cat: I Love My White Shoes	T	Pete the cat sings about his brand new white shoes as they change from red to blue to brown to wet.
Lobel, Anita	On Market Street	B	A child buys presents from A to Z in the shops along Market Street.
Lobel, Arnold	Frog and Toad Are Friends	P	Five tales recounting the adventures of two best friends—Frog and Toad.
London, Jonathan	Froggy Gets Dressed	P	Froggy wants to go out and play in the snow, but his mother keeps calling him in to dress him properly for the cold weather.
Martin, Bill	Brown Bear, Brown Bear, What Do You See?	T	Animal illustrations and captions provide an introduction to color concepts.
Martin, Bill	Chicka, Chicka Boom, Boom	T	When all the letters of the alphabet race up the coconut tree they worry it will be too full.
Mayer, Mercer	There's A Nightmare in My Closet	P	A young hero arms himself and awaits his rival, Nightmare.

Author	Title	Best for*	Synopsis
McBratney, Sam	Guess How Much I Love You?	B	Little Nutbrown Hare and his father, Big Nutbrown Hare take turns telling each other how much they love each other.
McCloskey, Robert	Blueberries for Sal	P	A little girl and a bear cub follow the wrong mothers as they pick blueberries.
McCloskey, Robert	Make Way for Ducklings	P	Mr. and Mrs. Mallard proudly return to their home in the Boston Public Garden with their eight offspring.
McGovern, Ann	Too Much Noise	P	Peter complains his house is too noisy until the wise man advises him to obtain some rather unusual house guests.
McKee, David	Elmer	P	Elmer, a patchwork of brilliant colors, gets tired of being different and making the other elephants laugh.
McKissack, Pat	Goin' Someplace Special	P	A young girl's story of growing up in the segregated South who longs to go where everyone is treated the same.
McMullan, Kate and Jim	I Stink!	P	A stinky night in the life of a New York City garbage truck and how he keeps the city clean.
McPhail, David	Pigs Aplenty, Pigs Galore	P	Pigs galore invade a house and have a wonderful party.
Meddaugh, Susan	Martha Speaks	P	Martha, the family dog, learns to speak after eating alphabet soup.
Mosel, Arlene	Tikki Tikki Tembo	P	A Chinese folk tale describes how the Chinese came to give all of their children short names after one boy falls into the well.
Munsch, Robert	The Paper Bag Princess	P	Princess Elizabeth is to marry Prince Ronald when a dragon attacks the castle and kidnaps Ronald. Elizabeth outsmarts the dragon and rescues Ronald But Ronald is unhappy by her un-princess-like appearance.

Author	Title	Best for*	Synopsis
Noble, Trinka	The Day Jimmy's Boa Ate the Wash	P	Jimmy's unusual pet accompanies him on his class trip to a farm.
Numeroff, Laura	If You Give a Mouse a Cookie	T	What will a mouse want after you give him a cookie?
Penn, Audrey	The Kissing Hand	P	Chester is reluctant to go to kindergarten for the first time, so his mother teaches him a secret way to carry her love with him.
Piper, Watty	The Little Engine that Could	P	The Little Blue Engine agrees to try to pull a stranded train full of toys over the mountain.
Potter, Beatrix	The Tale of Peter Rabbit	P	Peter disobeys his mother by going into Mr. McGregor's garden.
Rathmann, Peggy	Good Night, Gorilla	T	A mischievous little ape steals the zookeeper's keys and lets all the animals out of their cages.
Rey, H.A.	Curious George	P	The curiosity of a newly captured monkey gets him into continual trouble.
Rosen, Michael	We're Going on a Bear Hunt	T	Bear hunters go through grass, a river, mud, and other obstacles before their encounter with the bear forces a retreat.
Rylant, Cynthia	The Relatives Came	B	The relatives come to visit from Virginia and everyone has a wonderful time.
Scarry, Richard	Cars and Trucks and Things that Go	B	On their way to the beach for a picnic the Pig family encounters almost every kind of transportation vehicle.
Sendak, Maurice	Where the Wild Things Are	P	A naughty little boy, sent to bed without his supper, sails to the land of the wild things where he becomes their king.
Seuss, Dr.	Green Eggs and Ham	P	Sam-I-Am tries to persuade his friend to eat green eggs and ham.
Seuss, Dr.	How the Grinch Stole Christmas	P	The Grinch tries to stop Christmas from arriving by stealing all the presents and food from the village, but much to his surprise it comes anyway.

Author	Title	Best for*	Synopsis
Shaw, Charles	It Looked Like Spilt Milk	B	A continuously changing white cloud is silhouetted against a blue background for the reader to identify.
Shannon, David	No, David!	P	A young boy does a variety of naughty things for which he is reprimanded until he gets a hug.
Silverstein, Shel	The Giving Tree	P	A young boy grows to old age experiencing the love and generosity of a tree which gives to him without requiring anything in return.
Siomades, Lorianne	The Itsy Bitsy Spider	B	An illustrated version of the rhyme.
Slobodkina, Esphyr	Caps for Sale: a Tale of a Peddler, Some Monkeys, and Their Monkey Business	P	A band of mischievous monkeys steals every one of a peddler's caps while he takes a nap under a tree.
Steig, William	Sylvester and the Magic Pebble	P	Sylvester the donkey asks his magic pebble to turn him into a rock but then cannot hold the pebble to wish himself back to normal again.
Stevens, Janet	Tops and Bottoms	P	Hare turns his bad luck around by striking a clever deal with the rich and lazy bear down the road.
Stoeke, Janet	A Hat for Minerva Louise	T	Minerva Louise, a snow-loving chicken, mistakes a pair of mittens for two hats to keep both ends warm.
Taback, Simms	There Was an Old Lady Who Swallowed a Fly	P	The classic folk poem with illustrations on die-cut pages that reveal all that the old lady swallows.
Van Allsburg, Chris	The Polar Express	P	A magical train ride on Christmas Eve takes a boy to the North Pole to receive a special gift from Santa Claus.
Viorst, Judith	Alexander and the Terrible, Horrible, No Good, Very Bad Day	P	Everything goes wrong for Alexander but he is consoled by the thought that other people have bad days too.
Waddell, Martin	Owl Babies	T	Baby owls panic when they awaken one night and find their mother gone.

Author	Title	Best for*	Synopsis
Walsh, Ellen Stoll	Mouse Paint	T	Three white mice live on a piece of white paper so that the cat will not see them. They discover three jars of paint and blow their camouflage.
Waber, Bernard	Lyle, Lyle, Crocodile	P	Lyle is perfectly happy living with the Primms on East 88th Street in New York until Mr. Grumps next door changes all that.
Wells, Rosemary	Noisy Nora	P	Nora, the middle child, makes more and more noise to attract her parents' attention.
Wiesner, David	The Three Pigs	P	The three pigs escape the wolf by going into another world where they meet the cat and the fiddle, the cow that jumped over the moon, and a dragon.
Williams, Linda	The Little Old Lady Who Was Not Afraid of Anything	P	One windy autumn night, the little old lady who was not afraid of anything encounters a CLOMP, CLOMP in the woods.
Williams, Sue	I Went Walking	B	During the course of a walk, a young boy identifies animals of different colors.
Willems, Mo	Don't Let the Pigeon Drive the Bus	T	When the bus driver decides to take a break from driving, a wacky pigeon begs to take his place.
Willems, Mo	Knuffle Bunny: A Cautionary Tale	T	After Trixie and daddy leave the laundromat, Trixie's bunny turns up missing.
Wood, Audrey	The Napping House	T	A restless flea manages to wake up everyone in the house who was sleeping, including a mouse, cat, dog, boy, and his grandmother.
Yolen, Jane	Owl Moon	P	On a winter's night, a father and daughter trek into the woods to see the Great Horned Owl.

Author	Title	Best for*	Synopsis
Yolen, Jane	How do Dinosaurs Say Goodnight?	T	Mother and child ponder the different ways a dinosaur can say goodnight.
Zielinsky, Paul	Rumpelstiltskin	P	A strange little man helps the miller's daughter spin straw into gold for the king on the condition that she will give him her first-born child.
Zion, Gene	Harry, the Dirty Dog	P	When a white dog with black spots runs away from home, he gets so dirty his family doesn't recognize him when he returns home as a black dog with white spots.

* B = Baby, T = Toddler, P = Preschool.

Appendix D

Early Literacy Resources on the Web for Adults

While the American Academy of Pediatrics (AAP) recommends no television (or screen media such as computer games, videos, or DVDs) for children under two, it is unrealistic for us to ignore the magnitude of resources that surround us. The tools discussed in this chapter are always best accessed with a critical eye, keeping in mind that although children may learn some concepts from educational technology, they learn best from interactive, hands-on experiences with people they care about. The resources below are intended to guide caregivers in their journey to prepare their own children for their journey to kindergarten. As in all parenting decisions, common sense is the best guide.

—Early Literacy Resources for Adults

WEBSITES

Get Ready to Read! is for educators and parents of young children interested in the development of early literacy skills in the years before kindergarten. The site is a service of the National Center for Learning Disabilities. The resources and information provided on this site promote skill-building, communication between adults, and ways to address concerns. Under the "Early Literacy" tab, topics such as "Getting the Most Out of Picture Books," "Quality Television Shows That Focus on Early Literacy," "Get Ready to Read! Literacy Checklists," and "When Parents Are Concerned About Their Child's Early Learning Skills" are innovative. www.getreadytoread.org.

Get Set for K is a part of the Charlotte Mecklenburg Library's website. The month by month guide to school readiness offers parents and caregivers an early literacy skill to focus on for each month of the year. Then, they offer activity suggestions easy enough for every family to implement. While some suggestions are more appropriate for children in preschool, many can be used with babies and toddlers. www.cmlibrary.org/kids/getset4k.

Reach Out and Read is a nonprofit organization with a goal of promoting early literacy and school readiness. They focus on the medical field's involvement by giving new books to children when they visit their doctor's office. Through physician guidance they advocate for the importance of reading aloud.

Resources that can be found on their website and used by all parents include book suggestions, typical literacy milestones and recordings of classic children's books that can be streamed through the website. www.reachoutandread.org.

Reading Rockets is a national literacy initiative that offers information and resources on how young kids learn to read, why so many struggles, and how caring adults can help. Under the "Early Literacy Development" topic, visitors to the site can watch videos about literacy development, find activities to use with young children, explore the latest research on parent involvement in education, and much, much more. Literacy milestones from birth to age three are offered. www.readingrockets.org/atoz/early_literacy_development/.

Caroline Jackson Blakemore and Barbara Weston Ramirez, the authors of the website *Read To Your Baby*, are reading specialists. Together they have over fifty years helping elementary school children with reading difficulties. They instruct new parents in the field of emergent literacy and offer practical suggestions on how babies and toddlers will best achieve future school success. Specifically, they offer wonderful read aloud tips, resources and up to date research about babies and toddlers and their acquisition of language and literacy development. www.Readtoyourbaby.com.

Reading Is Fundamental (RIF) is the largest children's literacy nonprofit in the United States. The organization delivers free books and literacy resources to families who need them most. RIF provides new, free books for children to choose from and make their own. According to RIF, by providing children with books the children are empowered and motivated to see new possibilities. Highlights from their website includes the following:

- An *"Activities"* section that offer learning opportunities for every age group and skill level through cultural, dramatic, and writing activities.
- *"Booklists"* provide book suggestions by topic ranging from award winners to multicultural suggestions.
- The *"Articles"* section is full of ideas for teachers and parents wishing to encourage reading in new ways.
- The *"Brochures"* are easy-to-read guides offering tips for reading with young children and tips for selecting age appropriate books for youngsters. www.rif.org.

Rocky Mountain Public Broadcasting Services and Colorado Libraries for Early Literacy present *Storyblocks*. Storyblocks is a collection of thirty to sixty second videos which model for parents and caregivers songs, rhymes, and fingerplays appropriate for early childhood. Each video clip contains literacy tips to increase understanding of child development and preliteracy needs. The videos, in both English and Spanish are divided into three age ranges: babies (from birth to twenty-four months), toddlers (from two to three years), and preschoolers (from four to five years). www.storyblocks.org.

Jim Trelease is the author of million-copy bestseller, *The Read-Aloud Handbook*. Mr. Trelease has traveled to all fifty states and abroad, advocating the benefits of reading aloud to children. He has been recognized by both teachers and parents for his message that books are friends, not enemies. Sixty U.S. colleges use his *Handbook* as a text for education students. Korean, Chinese, Japanese, Indonesian, and Spanish editions of *The Read-Aloud Handbook* now reach parents and teachers worldwide. The useful website is chock full of information related to literacy. From discussions about reading education to the No Child Left Behind legislation and from booklists to research regarding the effects of television, Mr. Trelease's website covers it all. Free brochures and slides from his lectures are available for printing. Weekly read-aloud book reviews and a weekly essay from the author on current reading issues keep the site remarkably current. www.trelease-on-reading.com.

ZERO TO THREE is a nonprofit organization intent on informing, training, and supporting adults who are working to improve the lives of infants and toddlers. Their specific mission is to "promote the health and development of infants and toddlers." Their site is full of development charts, tips, and tools about child development, and tips regarding age-appropriate play. The site also offers information about school readiness and early literacy and language development. www.zerotothree.org

Read more at the authors own website: http://www.dawn-roginski.com/early-literacy-resources/.

Bibliography

Adams, M. *Beginning to Read: Thinking and Learning About Print*. Cambridge, MA: MIT Press, 1990.

Agee, Jon. *The Retired Kid*. New York: Hyperion Books for Children, 2008.

Alborough, Jez. *Hug*. Cambridge, MA: Candlewick Press, 2000.

Aliki. *My Visit to the Aquarium*. New York: HarperCollins, 1993.

Allard, Harry. *Miss Nelson Is Missing*. San Diego, CA: Houghton Mifflin, 1977.

Anderson, R., E. Hiebert, J. Scott, and I. Wilkinson. *Becoming a Nation of Readers: The Report of the Commission on Reading, U.S. Department of Education*. Champaign-Urbana, IL: Center for the Study of Reading, 1985.

Arnold, "Public Libraries and Early Literacy: Raising a Reader," *American Libraries* (2003): 48–51.

Asch, Frank. *Happy Birthday, Moon*. New York: Prentice-Hall, 1982.

———. *Pizza*. New York: Aladdin, 2015.

Aylesworth, Jim. *Old Black Fly*. New York: Holt, 1992.

Baker Keith. *Big Fat Hen*. San Diego, CA: Harcourt Brace, 1994.

Baker, L., and A. Wigfield. Dimensions of Children's Motivation for Reading and Their Relations to Reading Activity and Reading Achievement. *Reading Research Quarterly* (1997): 452–477.

Bang, Molly. *Ten, Nine, Eight*. New York: Greenwillow, 1983.

———. *When Sophie Gets Angry—Really, Really Angry*. New York: Blue Sky Press, 1999.

Barner, Bob. *Bugs, Bugs, Bugs*. San Francisco, CA: Chronicle Books, 1999.

Barney's Greatest Hits: The Early Years. Capitol Records, 2000. Sound Recording.

Barrett, Judi. *Cloudy With a Chance of Meatballs*. New York: Atheneum, 1978.

Bartels, Joanie. *Morning Magic*. Van Nuys, CA: BMG Music, 1987. Sound Recording.

Barton, Byron. *The Little Red Hen*. San Diego, CA: Houghton Mifflin/Clarion Books, 1973.

———. *Machines at Work*. New York: Crowell, 1987.

Beaty, Andrea. *Firefighter Ted*. New York: Margaret K. McElderry Books, 2009.

Beaumont, Karen. *I Ain't Gonna Paint No More!* Orlando, FL: Harcourt, 2005.

Bee, William. *Stanley's Garage.* New York: Peachtree, 2015.
———. *Stanley the Mailman.* New York: Peachtree, 2016.
Bemelmans, Ludwig. *Madeline.* New York: Puffin Books, 1939.
Berenstain, Jan. *The Berenstain Bears at the Aquarium.* New York: Harper, 2012.
Berry, Lynne. *Duck Tents.* New York: Henry Holt, 2009.
Bingham, Kelly. *Z is for Moose.* New York: Greenwillow Books, 2012.
Borass, Tracey. *Auto Mechanics.* Mankato, MN: Bridgestone Books, 1999.
Bourgeois, Paulette. *Franklin's School Play.* Toronto: Kids Can Press, 1996.
Boynton, Sandra. *Belly Button Book.* New York: Workman, 2005.
———. *Tickle Time!* New York: Workman, 2012.
Brett, Jan. *Goldilocks and the Three Bears.* New York: Penguin Group, 1992.
———. *The Mitten: A Ukrainian Folktale.* New York: Putnam, 1989.
Brisson, Pat. *Benny's Pennies.* New York: Doubleday Books for Young Readers, 1993.
Brown, Lisa. *The Airport Book.* New York: Roaring Book Press, 2016.
Brown, Marcia. *Stone Soup: An Old Tale.* New York: Scribner, 1947.
Brown, Margaret Wise. *Goodnight Moon.* New York: Harper & Row, 1947.
Bruce, Lisa. *Grow Flower, Grow! (Originally titled: Fran's Flower).* New York: Scholastic, 2001.
Brunhoff, Jean de. *The Story of Babar, the Little Elephant.* New York: Random House, 2002.
Buchman, Rachel. *Sing a Song of Seasons.* Cambridge, MA: Rounder Kids, 1997. Sound Recording.
Bunting, Eve. *The Butterfly House.* New York: Scholastic Press, 1999.
Burningham, John. *Mr. Gumpy's Outing.* New York: Henry Holt, 1970.
Burton, Virginia Lee. *Mike Mulligan and His Steam Shovel Story and Pictures.* San Diego, CA: Houghton Mifflin, 1939.
Buzzed, Toni. *One Cool Friend.* New York: Dial Books for Young Readers, 2012.
Cabrera, Jane. *Ten in the Bed.* New York: Holiday House, 2006.
Campbell, Rod. *Dear Zoo: A Lift the Flap Book.* New York: Little Simon, 2007.
Carle, Eric. *Draw Me a Star.* New York: Philomel Books, 1992.
———. *From Head to Toe.* New York: HarperCollins, 1997.
———. *The Very Hungry Caterpillar.* New York: Philomel Books, 1987.
Carlson, Nancy. *Start Saving, Henry!* New York: Viking, 2009.
Carter, Don. *Send It!* Brookfield, CN: Roaring Book Press, 2003.
Cash, Megan Montague. *I Saw the Sea and the Sea Saw Me.* New York: Viking, 2001.
Cedarmont Kid Singers. *100 Sing-Along-Songs for Kids.* Franklin, TN: Cedarmont Kids, 2007. Sound Recording.
Chernesky, Sanzari. *From Apple Trees to Cider, Please!* New York: Albert Whitman, 2015.
Christelow, Eileen. *Five Little Monkeys Jumping on the Bed.* New York: Clarion Books, 1989.
Church, Caroline Jayne. *Ten Tiny Toes.* New York: Cartwheel Books, 2014.
Cimarusti, Marie Torres. *Peek-a-Bloom.* New York: Dutton Children's Books, 2010.
Cooney, Barbara. *Miss Rumphius.* New York: Viking Press, 1982.
Cousins, Lucy. *Hooray for Fish!* Cambridge, MA: Candlewick Press, 2005.
———. *Maisy Goes Camping.* Cambridge, MA: Candlewick Press, 2004.
———. *Maisy's Show.* Somerville, MA: Candlewick Press, 2010.

Coyle, Carmela LaVigna. *Do Princesses Make Happy Campers?* New York: Taylor Trade, an imprint of Rowman & Littlefield, 2015.

Crews, Donald. *Freight Train.* New York: Greenwillow Books, 1978.

Cronin, Doreen. *Click, Clack, Moo Cows That Type.* New York: Simon & Schuster Books for Young Readers, 2000.

Darby, Kara. *Sing & Move.* Starkville, MS: Munchkin Musik Makers Productions, 2011. Sound Recording.

Darling-Hammand, Linda and Snyder, J. *Handbook of Research on Curriculum.* New York: MacMillan, 1992.

Daywalt, Drew. *The Day The Crayons Quit.* New York: Philomel Books, 2013.

Dean, James. *Pete the Cat: I Love My White Shoes.* New York: Harper, 2010.

de la Peña, Matt. *Last Stop on Market Street.* New York: GP Putnam's Sons, 2015.

DePaola, Tomie. *Strega Nona: an Old Tale.* New York: Prentice-Hall, 1975.

Dewdney, Anna. *Llama, Llama Mad At Mama.* New York: Viking, 2007.

———. *Llama, Llama Red Pajama.* New York: Penguin Group USA, 2015.

Diaper Gym: (Fun Activities for Babies On the Move). Long Branch, NJ: Kimbo Educational, 1985. Sound Recording.

Dines, Katherine. *Hunk-ta-bunk-ta wiggle. Volume One: 12 Tunes for Toddlers.* Denver, CO: Hunk-Ta-Bunk-Ta Music, 2006. Sound Recording.

DiPucchio, Kelly. *Gilbert Goldfish Wants a Pet.* New York: Dial Books for Young Readers, 2011.

Ditchfild, Christin. *Oil.* New York: Children's Press, 2002.

Downing, Johnette. *Music Time.* New Orleans, LA: Wiggle Worm Records, 2005. Sound Recording.

Downs, Mike. *The Noisy Airplane Ride.* Berkeley, CA: Tricycle Press, 2005.

Dunrea, Olivier. *Gossie.* Boston, MA: Houghton Mifflin, 2002.

Eastman, P.D. *Are You My Mother?* New York: Random House Books for Young Readers, 1960.

Ehlert. Lois. Fish Eyes: *A Book You Can Count On.* San Diego, CA: Harcourt Brace Jovanovich, 1990.

———. *Growing Vegetable Soup.* San Diego, CA: Harcourt Brace Jovanovich, 1987.

———. *Planting a Rainbow.* San Diego, CA: Harcourt Brace Jovanovich, 1988.

Ehrlich, Fred. *Does a Yak Get a Haircut?* Brooklyn, NY: Blue Apple Books, 2003.

Einhorn, Kama. *My First Book about Fish.* New York: Random House, 2006.

Emberley, Ed. *Go Away, Big Green Monster.* New York: Little Brown, 1992.

"Every Child Ready to Read," last modified 2015, http://everychildreadytoread.org.

"Every Child Ready to Read, 2nd edition Manual," last modified 2015, http://everychildreadytoread.org.

Falconer, Ian. *Olivia.* New York: Atheneum Books for Young Readers, 2000.

Feierabend, John Martin. *Frog in the Meadow: (Music, Now I'm Two).* Chicago, IL: GIA: 2000. Sound Recording.

———. *Ride Away on Your Horses: (Music, Now I'm One!)* Chicago, IL: GIA, 2000. Sound Recording.

Feiffer, Jules. *Bark George.* New York: HarperCollins, 1999.

Fielding, L. Kindergarten Learning Gap. *American School Board Journal* (April 2006): 32–34.

Finn, Rebecca, *Busy Fire Station.* New York: Sterling Children's Books, 2016.

Firestone, Mary. *Supermarket Managers.* Mankato, MN: Bridgestone Books, 2003.

Fleming, Denise. *Barnyard Banter.* New York: Holt, 1994.

———. *Lunch.* New York: Henry Holt, 1992.

———. *Mama Cat Has Three Kittens.* New York: Henry Holt, 1998.

Fletcher, Dave. *All of Two of Us.* CD Baby, 2012. http://www.cdbaby.com/cd/musicformoving.

Foley, Greg E. *Don't Worry Bear.* New York: Viking, 2008.

Fox, Mem. *Reading Magic.* San Diego, CA: Houghton Mifflin Harcourt, 2001.

Freedman, Claire. *Pirates Love Underpants.* New York: Aladdin, 2013.

Freeman, Don. *Corduroy.* New York: Viking Press, 1968.

Gag, Wanda. *Millions of Cats.* New York: Coward-McCann & Geoghegan, 1928.

Gaiman, Neil. *Chu's Day.* New York: Harper Collins Childrens, 2013.

Galdone, Paul. *The Gingerbread Boy.* San Diego, CA: Houghton Mifflin Harcourt, 2006.

———. *The Three Billy Goats Gruff.* San Diego, CA: Houghton Mifflin Harcourt, 1981.

———. *Three Little Kittens.* San Diego, CA: Houghton Mifflin Harcourt, 1988.

George, Lindsay Barrett. *That Pup.* New York: Greenwillow, 2011.

Gibbons, Gail. *Fill It Up! All About Service Stations.* New York: T.Y. Crowell, 1985.

Gil, Jim. *Jim Gill Sings the Sneezing Song and Other Contagious Tunes.* Oak Park, IL: Jim Gill Music, 2013. Sound Recording.

Gilkerson, J. and J. Richards. *The Power of Talk, 2nd edition.* The LENA Foundation (2009).

Goebel, Jenny. *The Firefighter.* New York: Grosset & Dunlap, an imprint of Penguin Group (USA), 2015.

Goldstein, M. Social Feedback to Infants' Babbling Facilitates Rapid Phonological Learning. *Psychological Science* (May 2008) 19: 515–523.

Graham, Bob. *Let's Get a Pup, said Kate.* Cambridge, MA: Candlewick Press, 2001.

Greene, Carol. *At the Grocery Store.* Chanhassen, MN: Child's World, 1999.

Guarina, Deborah. *Is Your Mama a Llama?* New York: Scholastic, 1989.

Hall, Zoe. *The Surprise Garden.* New York: Blue Sky Press, 1998.

Hammett, Carol Totsky. *It's Toddler Time.* Long Branch, NJ: Kimbo Educational 1982. Sound Recording.

———. *Preschool Action Time: Activities and Finger Plays.* Long Branch, NJ: Kimbo Educational, 1988.

———. *Toddlers on Parade: Musical Exercises for Infants and Toddlers.* Long Branch, NJ: Kimbo Educational, 1988.

Harrison, George H. *Backyard Bird Watching for Kids.* Minocqua, WI: Willow Creek Press, 1997.

Hart, Betty and Risley, T.R. *Meaningful Differences in the Everyday Experiences of Young American Children.* Baltimore, MD: Paul H. Brookes, 1995.

Healy, Jane. *Your Child's Growing Mind: Brain Development and Learning from Birth Through Adolescence.* New York: Broadway Books, 2004.

Hearn, Sam. *Busy Builders.* New York: Cartwheel Books, 2016.

Hegner, Priscilla A. *Baby Games.* Long Branch, NJ: Kimbo Educational, 1987. Sound Recording.

Heiligman, Deborah. *Fun Dog, Sun Dog.* New York: Marshall Cavendish, 2005.

Henkes, Kevin. *Chrysanthemum.* New York: Greenwillow Books, 1991.

———. *Lilly's Purple Plastic Purse.* New York: Greenwillow Books, 2006.

———. *Little White Rabbit.* New York: Greenwillow Books, 2011.

———. *Kitten's First Full Moon.* New York: Greenwillow Books, 2004.

Heo, Yumi. *Red Light, Green Light.* New York: Cartwheel Books, 2015.

Heos, Bridget. *Mustache Baby.* New York: Clarion Books, 2013.

Hill, Eric. *Spot's Harvest.* New York: G.P. Putnam's Sons, 2010.

———. *Where's Spot.* New York: Putnam, 1980.

Hills, Tad. *Duck and Goose.* New York: Schwartz & Wade Books, 2006.

Hillenbrand, Will. *Down By the Station.* San Diego, CA: Harcourt Brace, 1999.

Hoban, Russell. *Bread and Jam for Frances.* New York: HarperCollins, 1993.

Hoban, Tana. *I Read Symbols.* New York: Greenwillow Books, 1983.

Hoffman, Mary. *Amazing Grace.* New York: Dial Books for Young Readers, 1991.

Holabird, Katharine. *Angelina on Stage.* Middleton, WI: Pleasant Company, 2001.

Hubbell, Patricia. *Firefighters: Speeding! Spraying Saving!* Tarrytown, NY: Marshall Cavendish Children, 2007.

———. *My First Airplane Ride.* New York: Marshall Cavendish Children, 2008.

———. *Police: Hurrying! Helping! Saving!* Tarrytown, NY: Marshall Cavendish Children, 2008.

———. *Sea, Sand, Me!* New York: HarperCollins, 2001.

Huneck, Stephen. *Sally Goes to the Vet.* New York: Harry N. Abrams, 2004.

Hutchins, Hazel. *SNAP!* Toronto; New York: Vancouver: Annick Press, 2015.

Hutchins, Pat. *Good-Night, Owl!* New York: Macmillan, 1972.

———. *Rosie's Walk.* New York: Macmillan, 1968.

Jackson, Emma. *A Home for Dixie: The True Story of a Rescued Puppy.* New York: Collins, 2008.

Jeffers, Oliver. *The Heart and the Bottle.* New York: Philomel Books, 2010.

Johnson, Crockett. *Harold and the Purple Crayon.* New York: Harper, 1955.

Jones, Val. *Who Wants Broccoli?* New York: Harper Collins Children's Books, 2015.

Juster, T.F., F. Stafford, and H. Ono. Major Changes Have Taken Place in How Children and Teens Spend Their Time. *Child Development Supplement* (2004).

Kagan, J., N. Herschkowitz, and E. Herschkowitz. *A Young Mind in a Growing Brain.* Mahwah, NJ: Lawrence Erlbaum Associates, 2005.

Kann, Victoria. *Pinkalicious.* New York: HarperCollins, 2006.

Kasza, Keiko. *The Wolf's Chicken Stew.* New York: Putnam, 1987.

Katz, Karen. *Counting Kisses.* New York: Little Simon, 2010.

———. *Zoom, Zoom, Baby.* New York: Little Simon, 2014.

Kaye, Danny. *A Child's Celebration of Song.* Redway, CA: Music for Little People, 1992. Sound Recording.

Keats, Ezra Jack. *Snowy Day.* New York: Puffin Books, 1962.

Kimmel, Eric. *Anansi and the Moss Covered Rock.* New York: Holiday House, 1988.

Kraus, Ruth. *The Carrot Seed.* New York: Harper & Row, 1945.

Kuhl, P.K., K.A. Williams, F. Lacerda, K.N. Stevens, and B. Lindblom. Linguistic Experience Alters Phonetic Perception in Infants by 6 Months of Age. *Science* (1992): 606–608.

Lakin, Patricia. *Camping Day.* New York: Dial Books for Young Readers, 2009.

Lakritz, Deborah. *Say Hello, Lily.* Minneapolis, MN: Kat-Ben Pub, 2010.

Landau, Orna. *Leopardpox.* New York: Clarion Books, Houghton Mifflin Harcourt, 2014.

Leaf, Munro. *The Story of Ferdinand.* New York: Viking Press, 1964.

Learning Station. *Kids Nursery Rhymes. Volume 1.* US: MasterSong, 2001. Sound Recording.

———. *Get Funky and Musical Fun with the Learning Station.* Melbourne, FL: Learning Station, 2003. Sound Recording.

———. *Teach a Toddler: Playful Songs for Learning.* Long Branch, NJ: Kimbo Educational, 1985. Sound Recording.

Lee, Chinlun. *Good Dog, Paw.* Cambridge, MA: Candlewick Press, 2004.

Leonard, Marcia. *The Pet Vet.* Brookfield, CT: Millbrook Press, 1999.

Lerner, Carol. *Butterflies in the Garden.* New York: Harper Collins, 2002.

Liberman, I.Y., D. Shankweiler, and A.M. Liberman. The Alphabetic Principle and Learning to Read. Haskin Laboratories Status Report on Speech Research (1990).

Lionni, Leo. *Swimmy.* New York: Pantheon, 1963.

Litwin, Eric. *Pete the Cat: I Love My White Shoes.* New York: Harper, 2008.

Lobel, Anita. *On Market Street.* New York: Greenwillow Books, 1981.

Lobel, Arnold. *Frog and Toad Are Friends.* New York: Harper & Row, 1970.

Lombardi, Kristine A. *The Grumpy Pets.* New York: Abrams Books for Young Readers, 2016.

London, Jonathan. *Froggy Gets Dressed.* New York: Viking, 1992.

———. *A Plane Goes Ka-Zoom.* New York: Henry Holt, 2010.

Long, Melinda. *How I Became a Pirate.* San Diego, CA: Harcourt, 2003.

Maccarone, Grace. *I Shop With My Daddy.* New York: Scholastic, 1998

Mangina, C., and E. Sokolov. Neuronal Plasticity in Memory and Learning Abilities: Theoretical Position and Selective Review. *International Journal of Psychophysiology* (2006): 203–214.

Marshall, James. *Red Riding Hood.* New York: Penguin Group, 1987.

Martin Jr, Bill. *Chicka Chicka Boom Boom.* New York: Beach Lane Books, 2009.

———. *Brown Bear, Brown Bear, What Do You See?* New York: Henry Holt, 1996.

Mayer, Mercer. *There's A Nightmare in My Closet.* New York: Dial Press, 1968.

McBratney, Sam. *Guess How Much I Love You.* Somerville, MA: Candlewick Press, 1994.

McCloskey, Robert. *Blueberries for Sal.* New York: Viking Press, 1948.

———. *Make Way for Ducklings.* New York: Viking Press, 1941.

McGovern, Ann. *Too Much Noise.* San Diego, CA: Houghton Mifflin, 1992.

McGrath, Bob. *Sing Along with Bob #1.* Teaneck, NJ: Bob's Kids Music, 2000. Sound Recording.

McKee, David. *Elmer.* New York: Lothrop, Lee & Shepard Books, 1968.

McKissack, Pat. *Goin' Someplace Special.* New York: Atheneum Books for Young Readers, 2001.

McMullen, Kate and Jim. *I Stink!* New York: Joanna Cotler Books, 2002.

McMullan, Kate and Jim. *I Stink!* New York: Joanne Cotler Books, 2002.

McPhail, David. *Pigs Aplenty, Pigs Galore.* New York: Dutton Children's Books, 1993.

McQuin, Anna. *Lola Plants a Garden.* Watertown, MA: Charlesbridge, 2014.

Meadows, Michelle. *Traffic Pups.* New York: Simon & Schuster Books for Young Readers, 2011.

Meddaugh, Susan. *Martha Speaks.* San Diego, CA: Houghton Mifflin, 1992.

Miller, Margaret. *What's On My Head?* New York: Little Simon, 2009.

Miller, Virginia. *Ten Red Apples.* Cambridge, MA: Candlewick Press, 2002.

Minden, Cecilia. *Letter Carriers.* Chanhassen, MN: Child's World, 2006.

———. *Veterinarians.* Chanhassen, MN: Child's World, 2014.

Montenegro, Laura Nyman. *A Poet's Bird Garden.* New York: Farrar Straus Girouz, 2007.

More Silly Songs. Burbank, CA: Walt Disney Records, 1998. Sound Recording.

Mosel, Arlene. *Tikki, Tikki Tembo.* New York: Holt, Rinehart and Winston, 1968.

Moss, Miriam. *Bad Hare Day.* New York: Bloomsbury Books: Distributed to the trade by Holtzbink, 2003.

Munsch, Robert. *The Paper Bag Princess.* New York: Annick Press, 1980.

Music for Moving. *Preschool Action Songs 2 (Ages 3–7); Pre-K & Kindergarten Music for Young Children,* 2013. http://www.cdbaby.com/cd/musicformoving.

National Institute for Literacy. *Fast Facts on Literacy & Fact Sheet on Correctional Education.* Washington DC, 1998.

National Research Council. *Preventing Reading Difficulties in Young Children.* Washington DC: National Research Council, 1998.

Noble, Trinka. *The Day Jimmy's Boa Ate the Wash.* New York: Dial Press, 1980.

Numeroff, Laura Joffe. *If You Give a Mouse a Cookie.* New York: HarperCollins, 1985.

Nowakowski, R. Stable Neuron Numbers From Cradle to Grave. *Proceedings of the National Academy of Sciences of the United States of America* (2006): 12219–12220.

O'Connor, Jane. *Fancy Nancy.* New York: Harper, 2006.

Okie, Iona. *Snuggle Up With Mother Goose.* Somerville, MA: Candlewick Press, 2015.

Orloff, Karen Kaufman. *I Wanna Go Home.* New York: G. P. Putnam's Sons, an imprint of Penguin Group (USA), 2014.

Oxley, Jennifer. *Peg & Cat: the Pizza Problem.* Cambridge, MA: Candlewick Entertainment, 2016.

Palmer, Hap. *Peek-A-Boo: and Other Songs for Young Children.* Topanga, CA: Hap-Pal Music, 1997. Sound Recording.

———. *Two Little Sounds: Fun with Phonics and Numbers.* Topanga, CA: Hap-Pal Music, 2003. Sound Recording.

———. *Walter the Waltzing Worm.* Freeport, NY: Activity Records, 1982. Sound Recording.

Parsley, Elise. *If You Ever Want to Bring a Piano to the Beach, Don't!* New York: Little, Brown, 2016.

Pat the Bunny at the Apple Orchard. New York: Golden Books, an imprint of Random House Children's Books, 2015.

Penn, Audrey. *The Kissing Hand.* New York: The Child Welfare League of America, 1993.

Peterson, Carole. *Dancing Feet.* [United States]: Macaroni Soup, 2008. Sound Recording.

———. *H. U. M. All Year Long: Highly Usable Music Kids Can Sing, Dance & Do.* [United States]: Macaroni Soup, 2003. Sound Recording.

———. *Season Sings!* [United States]: Macaroni Soup, 2012. Sound Recording.

———. *Sticky Bubble Gum and Other Tasty Tunes: Sing Along, Dance Along, Do Along.* [United States]: Macaroni Soup, 2003. Sound Recording.

Piggyback Songs: Singable Poems Set to Favorite Tunes. Long Branch, NJ: Kimbo, 1995. Sound Recording.

Piper, Watty. *The Little Engine That Could.* New York: Platt & Munk, 1976.

Pfister, Marcus. *Rainbow Fish.* New York: North-South Books, 1992.

Potter, Beatrix. *The Tale of Peter Rabbit.* New York: Viking Penguin, 1902.

Poydar, Nancy. *Mailbox Magic.* New York: Holiday House, 2000.

Raffi. *Down By The Bay.* New York: Crown, 1987.

———. *One Light, One Sun.* Willowdale, ON: Shoreline Records ; Cambridge, MA: Distributed by Rounder Records, [1996], 1985. Sound Recording.

Rathmann, Peggy. *Good Night, Gorilla.* New York: Puffin Books, 2000.

Ready, Jean. *Busy Builders, Busy Week!* New York: Bloomsbury Children's Books, 2016.

Rey, H.A. *Curious George.* San Diego, CA: Houghton Mifflin, 1941.

Rim, Sujean, *Birdie's Big-Girl Hair.* Boston, MA: Little, Brown, 2014.

Rockwell, Anne. *At the Firehouse.* New York: HarperCollins, 2003.

———. *Our Stars.* San Diego, C: Silver Whistle, 1999.

Rosen, Michael. *We're Going On a Bear Hunt.* New York: Margaret K. McElderry Books, 1989.

Rosenberry, Vera. *Who Is In the Garden?* New York: Holiday House, 2001.

Rossetti-Shustak, Bernadette. *I Love You Through and Through.* New York: Cartwheel Books, 2005.

Rowe, M.L., K.A. Leech, and N. Cabrera. Going Beyond Input Quantity: Wh-Questions Matter for Toddlers' Language and Cognitive Development. *Cognitive Science* (2016): 162–179.

Russia, Sergio. *Bear and Bee.* New York: Disney Hyperion Books, 2013.

Rylant, Cynthia. *The Great Gracie Chase: Stop That Dog.* New York: Blue Sky Press, 2001.

———. *The Relatives Came.* New York: Bradbury Press, 1985.

Sauer, Tammi. *I Love Cake!: Starring Rabbit, Porcupine, and Moose.* New York: Katherine Tegan Books, 2016.

Savadier, Elivia. *No Haircut Today.* New Milford, CT: Roaring Book Press, 2005.

Savage, Stephen. *The Mixed-Up Truck.* New York: Roaring Brook Press, 2016.

Scarry, Richard. *Cars and Trucks and Things That Go.* New York: Golden Press, 1974.

Schertle, Alice. *All You Need for a Beach.* Orlando, FL: Silver Whistle/Harcourt, 2004.

Searcy, John. *Signs in our World.* London: DK Children, 2006.

Seltzer, Lynn. *The Construction Crew.* New York: Henry Holt, 2011.

Sendak, Maurice. *Where The Wild Things Are.* New York: HarperCollins, 1963.

Seuss, Dr. *Green Eggs and Ham.* New York: Beginner Books, 1960.

———. *How The Grinch Stole Christmas.* New York: Random House, 1957.

Shannon, David. *Duck on a Bike.* New York: Blue Sky Press, 2002.

———. *No, David!* New York: Blue Sky Press, 1998.

Shaw, Charles Green. *It Looked Like Spilt Milk.* New York: HarperCollins, 1947.

Shore, Rima. *Rethinking the Brain: New Insights Into Early Development.* New York: Families and Work Institute, 1997.

Shulman, Mark. *Gorilla Garage.* New York: Marshall Cavendish, 2009.

Silverstein, Shel. *The Giving Tree.* New York: Harper & Row, 1964.

Simon, Charnan. *Police Officers.* Chanhassen, MN: Child's World, 2003.

Singer, Marilyn. *I'm Gonna Climb a Mountain in My Patent Leather Shoes.* New York: Abrams Books for Young Readers, 2014.

Siomades, Lorianne. *The Itsy Bitsy Spider.* New York: Boyds Mills Press, 1999.

Siomades, Lorianne. *Itsy Bitsy Spider.* Honesdale, PA: Boyds Mills Press, 1999.

Sirimarco, Elizabeth. *At the Bank.* Chanhassen, MN: Child's World, 2000.

———. *At the Barber.* Eden Prairie, MN: Child's World, 2000.

Sloane, Shari. *Singing with Shari: Oldies but Goodies.* 2013. http://www.cdbaby.com/cd/sharisloane3.

Slobodkina, Sephyr. *Caps for Sale: A Tale of a Peddler, Some Monkeys and Their MonkeyBusiness.* New York: HarperCollins, 1968.

Snow, C., M. Burns, and P. Griffin. *Preventing Reading Difficulties in Young Children.* Washington DC: National Academy Press, 1998.

Staniford, Linda. *Police to the Rescue Around the World.* New York: Heinemann Raintree, 2016.

Steers, Billy. *Tractor Mac: Teamwork.* New York: Farrar Straus Giroux, 2016.

Steig, William. *Pete's a Pizza.* New York: HarperCollins, 1998.

———. *Sylvester and the Magic Pebble.* New York: Simon & Schuster Books for Young Readers, 1997.

Stevens, Janet. *The Princess and the Pea.* New York: Holiday House, 1989.

———. *Tops and Bottoms.* New York: Harcourt Brace, 1995.

Stewart, Georgiana Liccione. *Action Songs for Preschoolers: a Treasury of Fun.* Long Branch, NJ: Kimbo Educational, 2003. Sound Recording.

———. *Baby Face.* Long Branch, NJ: Kimbo Educational, 1983. Sound Recording.

Stoeke, Janet Morgan. *A Hat for Minerva Louise.* New York: Dutton Children's Books, 1994

Strauss, R.S., D. Rodzilsky, G. Burack, and M. Colin, Psychosocial Correlates of Physical Activity in Healthy Children, *Archive of Pediatric and Adolescent Medicine* (2001): 155, 897–902.

Strickland, Paul. *Dinosaur Roar.* New York: Puffin Books, 1994.

Sturges, *I Love Trains!* New York: HarperCollins, 2001.

Suen, Anastasia. *Window Music.* New York: Viking, 1998.

Sullivan, Mary. *Ball.* New York: Houghton Mifflin Harcourt, 2016.

Sunseri, MaryLee. *Baby-O!* Pacific Grove, CA: Piper Grove Music, 2005. Sound Recording.

Suskind, Dana. *Thirty-Million Words: Building a Child's Brain.* New York: Dutton, 2015.

Taback, Simms. *I Miss You Every Day.* New York: Viking, 2007.

———. *There Was an Old Lady Who Swallowed a Fly.* New York: Viking, 1997.

Tafuri, Nancy. *All Kinds of Kisses.* New York: LB Kids, 2014.

———. *Blue Goose.* New York: Simon & Schuster Books for Young Readers, 2008.

———. *Will You Be My Friend? A Bunny and Bird Story.* New York: Scholastic Press, 2000.

Teckentrup, Britta. *Get Out of My Bath.* Somerville, MA: Nosy Crow, 2015.

Trapani, Iza. *Twinkle, Twinkle Little Star.* Boston, MA: Whispering Coyote Press, 1994.

Trelease, Jim. *Why Read Aloud to Children.* Last modified 2014, http://treleaseonreading.com.

"Trelease on Reading," last modified 2014, http://trelease-on-reading.com.

Underwood, Deborah. *Good Night, Baddies.* New York: Beach Lane Books, 2016.

Valeri, Michele. *Little Ditties for Itty Bitties.* Community Music, 2010. Sound Recording.

Van Allsburg, Chris. *The Polar Express.* New York: Houghton Mifflin, 1985.

Van Lieshout, Maria. *Backseat A-B-see.* San Francisco, CA: Chronicle Books, 2012.

Viorst, Judith. *Alexander and the Terrible, Horrible, No Good, Very Bad Day.*

Waber, Bernard. *Lyle, Lyle Crocodile.* New York: Houghton Mifflin, 1965.

Waddell. Martin. *Owl Babies.* Cambridge, MA: Candlewick Press, 1992.

Wallace, Nancy Elizabeth. *Apples, Apples, Apples.* Delray Beach, FL: Winslow Press, 2000.

Walsh, Ellen Stoll. *Mouse Paint.* San Diego, CA: Harcourt Brace Jovanovich, 1989.

Walsh, Melanie. *Monster, Monster.* Cambridge, MA: Candlewick Press, 2002.

Walter, Virginia. *"Hi" Pizza Man.* New York: Orchard Books, 1995.

Watt, Fiona. *That's Not My Series (Usborne Touchy-Feely Books).* Wokingham, UK: Osborne Books, 2002–2010.

Weikart, P.S., L.J. Schweinhart, and M. Larner. Movement Curriculum Improves Children's Rhythmic Competence. *HighScope ReSource* (1987): 8–10.

Wellington, Monica. *Pizza at Sally's.* New York: Dutton Children's Books, 2006.

———. *Zinnia's Flower Garden.* New York: Dutton Children's Books, 2005.

Wells, Rosemary. *Bunny Money.* New York: Dial Books for Young Readers, 1997.

———. *Noisy Nora.* New York: Dial Books for Young Readers, 1997.

Wiesner, David. *The Three Pigs.* New York: Clarion Books, 2001.

Wiggles. *Racing to the Rainbow.* New York: Koch Records, 2007. Sound Recording.

Willems, Mo. *Don't Let the Pigeon Drive the Bus!* New York: Hyperion Books for Children, 2003.

———. *Elephant & Piggie Books.* New York: Disney Hyperion, 2007-2016.

———. *Knuffle Bunny: A Cautionary Tale.* New York: Hyperion Books for Children, 2004.

Williams, Sue. *I Went Walking.* San Diego, CA: Harcourt Brace Jovanovich, 1989.

Wilson, Steve. *Hedgehugs.* New York: Henry Holt, 2015.

Wonder Kids Choir. *Favorite Sing-A-Longs. Volumes 1–3.* St. Laurent, Quebec, Canada: Madacy Entertainment Group, 2000. Sound Recording.

Wood, Don. *The Little Mouse, the Red Ripe Strawberry and the Big Hungry Bear.* New York: Child's Play (International), 1984.

———. *The Napping House.* San Diego, CA: Harcourt Brace Jovanovich, 1984.

———. *Piggies.* San Diego, CA: Harcourt Brace Jovanovich, 1991.

Yolen, Jane. *How Do Dinosaurs Say Goodnight?* New York: Blue Sky Press, 2000.

———. *Owl Moon.* New York: Philomel Books, 1987.

Zielinsky, Paul. *Rumpelstilskin.* New York: E.P. Dutton, 1986.

Zion, Gene. *Harry, the Dirty Dog.* New York: Harper, 1956.

Zolotow, Charlotte. *I Know a Lady.* New York: Greenwillow, 1984.

About the Author

Dawn Roginski is the early childhood outreach librarian at Medina County District Library (Ohio). She visits more than thirty day cares and preschools throughout Medina County sharing stories, music, movement, and mini-lessons. Prior to joining the Medina County District Library, Roginski spent ten years as the children's librarian for Cuyahoga County Public Library in Chagrin Falls (Ohio).

She obtained both her master's degree in library and information science and her undergraduate degree in elementary education from Kent State University. She has returned to Kent State University this year to begin the pursuit of her PhD in curriculum and instruction with a focus on literacy. She continues to hold an active teaching license in the state of Ohio.

Roginski is a member of the American Library Association Services to Children division (ALSC), the Ohio Library Council (OLC), and the National Association for the Education of Young Children (NAEYC). She holds a seat on the County Career Center advisory board where she works to educate future early-childhood educators in the best practices for early literacy.

She published the best of her library storytimes in 2014. She maintains an active speaking schedule and looks forward to her time discussing the critical years of zero to five with educators, librarians, parents, and all who love to lead learning for our littlest learners.

The children referred to in this book are Rachel (21), Leah (19), and Alex (12) Roginski. Both girls are students at Xavier University while their brother Alex is busy with middle school and baseball.

Ms. Roginski enjoys spending her free time reading picture books for young children and scrapbooking her fondest parenting moments. She is engaged to be married. She lives in North Royalton (Ohio) with her fiancé, children, and two crazy mutts (Tootsie and Misty).